ADD ANOTHER PLACE SETTING

Recipes from the
JUNIOR LEAGUE OF
NORTHWEST ARKANSAS

Add Another Place Setting

Published by the Junior League of Northwest Arkansas
614 E. Emma, Suite M432, Springdale, AR 72764

Copyright © 2008 by Junior League of Northwest Arkansas

Photography copyright © by Joe Wittkop Photography, Inc.
Food styling by Derek Nacey

Library of Congress Control Number: 2007929333
ISBN: 978-0-9790769-0-9

Edited, Designed, and Manufactured by
Favorite Recipes® Press
An imprint of

FRP

P. O. Box 305142
Nashville, Tennessee 37230
800-358-0560

Art Director: Steve Newman
Book Design: Bruce Gore
Project Editor: Nicki Pendleton Wood

Manufactured in China
First Printing: 2008
10,000 copies

Proceeds from the sale of this book will support the ongoing
projects and programs of the Junior League of Northwest Arkansas,
a nonprofit organization of women committed to promoting voluntarism,
developing the potential of women and improving communities
through effective action and leadership of trained volunteers.

We're delighted to present our first cookbook, *Add Another Place Setting*. In the realm of Junior Leagues, compiling a cookbook is a coming-of-age project.

In 1992 I was the first president of the organization that was to become the Junior League of Northwest Arkansas (JLNWA). At that time, my husband and I had four daughters at home, ages ranging from twelve to two. Fast forward and the two-year-old is sixteen, driving, and our only full-time resident. The organization that became JLNWA now has more than three hundred members. A careful determination was made that we were ready and able to launch a cookbook, and I was honored to be asked to chair the Cookbook Committee.

Northwest Arkansas has been my home for more than twenty years. My husband and I love this wonderful place. Good food and good cooks are an integral part of our area. Entertaining is comfortable and easy. I knew we—the League and Cookbook Committee—could do this.

I've always thought of myself as a domestic feminist. I've spent time at home rearing our daughters, but volunteering was a way I could continue to "work," yet maintain control of my time. When our daughters were young, any time we would find ourselves faced with a difficult situation I would raise the question—as a coach would—"Are we girls or are we women?" The answer would come back, in young, sweet voices I can still hear, "We are women!" By taking on a cookbook project, Junior League of Northwest Arkansas has figuratively asked its members that same question. We've responded in a united, strong voice. Not only are we women, we're women who can cook.

Thank you for your interest in *Add Another Place Setting*. We hope you enjoy our "cook's tour" of Northwest Arkansas.

∽∾

SUSAN FOUNTAIN HUI
Past President and Chair, Cookbook Committee
Junior League of Northwest Arkansas

MISSION STATEMENT

The Junior League of Northwest Arkansas is an organization of women committed to promoting voluntarism, developing the potential of women, and improving communities through the effective action and leadership of trained volunteers. Its purpose is exclusively educational and charitable.

REACHING OUT STATEMENT

The Junior League of Northwest Arkansas reaches out to women of all races, religions, and national origins who demonstrate an interest in and commitment to voluntarism.

LEAGUE HISTORY

Established in 1992, the Junior League of Northwest Arkansas affiliated with the Association of Junior Leagues International in 1999. The Junior League of Northwest Arkansas has been recognized at the national and local levels for outstanding volunteer service as a recipient of the USA Today/Paul Newman Community Service Award and the Association of Junior Leagues International's Award for Outstanding Strategic Planning, as well as Northwest Arkansas Business Journal's Nonprofit Organization of the Year and Outstanding Volunteer Service Organization by the Fayetteville Chamber of Commerce. The three hundred members of the Junior League of Northwest Arkansas contribute over thirty-five thousand hours of volunteer service to community organizations in Northwest Arkansas each year.

PROJECTS AND INITIATIVES OF THE JUNIOR LEAGUE OF NORTHWEST ARKANSAS

Arkansas Athlete's Outreach

Art from the Heart

Art in Schools

Back to School Backpacks

Children's House

Children's Safety Center Toy Room

Christmas Baskets for Families

Clothes Closet

Coaching Boys into Men

Domestic Violence Campaign

Cooperative Emergency Outreach

Crayola DreamMakers

Discovery Room Museum

Earth Day

Fabergé Ball

Fun Friends at Bates Elementary

Gumbo Ya-Ya

Havenwood

Head Start

HealthCare Action

Hurricane Katrina Relief Project

A Mile in My Shoes

Northwest Arkansas Children's Shelter

Ozark Food Bank

Ozark Race for the Cure

Peace at Home Family Shelter

Project Kids Hope

Public Affairs Committee

Real Women Project

Restoration Village

Rhythm and Blues

Serve Our Shelters

Scheherezade

Shop with a Cop

Single Parent Scholarship Fund

Tell Tale Readers

That's My Bag Project

Touch a Truck

Winter Dreams Tour of Homes

Women's Independence Network

CONTENTS

MENUS

Whole Hog

Whether it's football, basketball, track, or baseball,
when the Razorbacks play in Fayetteville, we know they're home.

———

Tailgate Corn Bread Salad 102

Game Day Cheese Dip 78

Football Season Muffulettas 129

Foolproof Baked Brisket 110

Cinnamon Pecans 87

Sugar Pecan Crisps 169

Fall Outdoors

Autumn in the Ozarks is one of the most beautiful seasons, with several entertaining options. Craft fairs, Oktoberfest, and hiking in Devil's Den are among our many choices. Here is a menu idea for a crisp afternoon.

——————

AUTUMN BRIE WITH FRUIT AND NUTS 81

BEEF BREAD BOWL DIP 77

OZARK POTATO SALAD 102

WEEKEND NAVY BEANS AND HAM 128

FALL COLOR PUMPKIN DIP 81

FROSTY MUG ROOT BEER 90

Ladies' Luncheon

*For generations of Southern women, a bridal shower
or ladies' luncheon is an occasion for your best linen, china,
and silver. Celebrate the tradition and enjoy a spring
or early summer afternoon with these recipes.*

CHICKEN POPPY SEED PASTA SALAD 100

GEN BROYLES'S REFRIGERATOR ROLLS 73

BERNICE JONES'S BRIDGE CLUB PIE 167

CRANBERRY TEA 88

Commencement

*An end, a beginning—commencement is a time
to celebrate. In Northwest Arkansas, red is the color of the day
for the University of Arkansas.*

——————

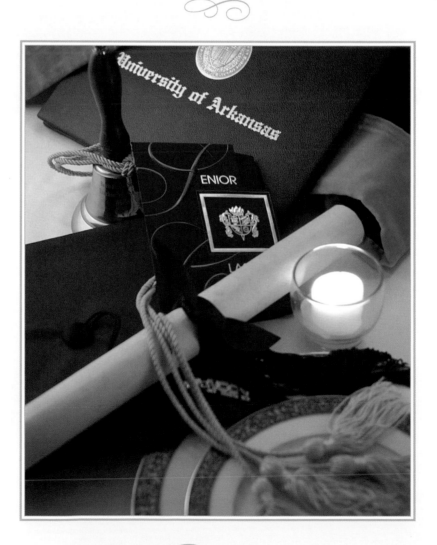

Gala Afterglow

A midnight breakfast is an elegant way to end an evening or begin a new year.
Your guests will enjoy the following dishes.

———

CAPPUCCINO MUFFINS WITH ESPRESSO TOPPING 66

CRANBERRY FRENCH TOAST 63

FIERY BREAKFAST CASSEROLE 58

SPICY CHEESE GRITS 61

FRESH FRUIT

Company's Here

The doorbell rings just as the table is being set.
Another place setting is added, and company's here for dinner.
Welcome guests to your home with comfort food.

————

COMPANY'S COMING WHITE LASAGNA 123

BACON AND MANDARIN SALAD 104

CHOCOLATE COBBLER 163

Book Club

Book clubs abound in this area. Welcome literary guests to your home with these menu ideas for book club fare.

———

SMOKED SALMON FINGER SANDWICHES 85

STRAWBERRY SPINACH SALAD 104

TONTITOWN CREAM CAKE 159

SWEET DIP FOR FRESH FRUIT 80

MOCHA PUNCH 88

FARMERS' MARKET

Fresh Fruits and Vegetables

Asparagus with Pesto Tomatoes 18

Sautéed Green Beans
with Corn 18

Green Beans with Ginger 19

Salade Liegeoise 20

Green Bean, Tomato and
Potato Salad 21

Crustless Summer Squash
Quiche 22

Southern Squash Casserole 22

Bentonville Farmers' Market
Tomatoes 23

Town Square Tomatoes 23

Tomatoes Vinaigrette 24

Fresh Salsa 24

Spinach-Stuffed Zucchini 25

Tomato Relish 25

Bread and Butter Pickles 26

Fayetteville Farmers' Market
Pesto 26

Apple Orchard Cake 27

Fresh Apple Muffins 27

Big Red Apple Shortcake 28

Apple Butter 28

Apple Bread Pudding with
Vanilla Sauce 29

Sour Cream Blueberry Pie 32

Blueberry Streusel Bread 32

Blueberry Bread with
Vanilla Sauce 33

Asparagus with Pesto Tomatoes

1	pound fresh asparagus, trimmed	1/4	cup basil pesto
2	tablespoons butter	2	tablespoons grated Parmesan cheese
1	cup chopped cherry tomatoes		

Add the asparagus to a large saucepan of boiling water and boil for 4 to 5 minutes; drain. Add the butter to the asparagus and toss until the butter is melted. Combine the tomatoes, pesto and cheese in a bowl and mix gently. Arrange the asparagus on a serving platter and top with the tomato mixture.

MAKES 4 TO 6 SERVINGS

Sautéed Green Beans with Corn

3	pounds green beans, trimmed and cut into 2-inch pieces	2	cups fresh corn kernels or frozen corn kernels, thawed
3	tablespoons butter		Salt and pepper to taste
1/4	cup thinly sliced shallots or small white onions	5 to	6 teaspoons chopped fresh herbs such as dill weed, parsley, tarragon and thyme
1	large red bell pepper, chopped		

Cook the beans in a saucepan of boiling water until tender-crisp; drain. Melt the butter in a skillet. Add the shallots and bell pepper and sauté over medium-high heat for 3 minutes or just until tender. Add the beans and corn and sauté for 2 minutes or until heated through. Season with salt and pepper. Add half the herbs to the bean mixture and mix well. Remove to a serving dish and sprinkle with the remaining herbs.

MAKES 8 SERVINGS

Green Beans with Ginger

1	pound fresh green beans, trimmed
2	green onions, chopped
2	garlic cloves, minced
2 to	3 teaspoons minced fresh ginger
2	tablespoons sesame oil
1/2	cup roasted red bell pepper, thinly sliced
1	tablespoon oyster sauce
1/8	teaspoon pepper
1/4	cup slivered almonds, toasted

Cook the beans in a saucepan of boiling water for 4 to 6 minutes or until tender-crisp; drain. Plunge the beans into ice water to stop the cooking process; drain. Sauté the green onions, garlic and ginger in the sesame oil in a large nonstick skillet over medium heat for 1 minute. Add the beans and bell pepper and sauté for 1 minute. Stir in the oyster sauce and pepper. Cook until heated through, stirring constantly. Sprinkle with the almonds and serve.

MAKES 6 TO 8 SERVINGS

Salade Liegeoise

The warm bacon and vinegar dressing is also good on a mixture of leafy and bitter salad greens.

6 to	8 new potatoes (red, Yukon Gold or fingerlings)
	Salt to taste
1	pound fresh green beans, trimmed
4	ounces lean bacon, cut into 1/4-inch pieces
1/4	cup red wine vinegar
1	tablespoon sugar
2	shallots, or 1 small onion, minced
1	tablespoon chopped fresh dill weed or 1/4 cup chopped fresh parsley
	Pepper to taste

Cook the potatoes in a saucepan of boiling salted water for 20 minutes or until tender; drain. Heat in the pan for 1 minute to dry, tossing constantly. Peel the potatoes and keep warm. Cook the beans in a saucepan of boiling salted water just until tender-crisp. Drain and add to the potatoes. Fry the bacon in a skillet until crisp. Pour the bacon and bacon drippings over the potatoes and beans. Add the wine vinegar to the skillet and deglaze the skillet. Add the sugar and cook for 1 minute, stirring constantly. Pour over the bean mixture. Add the shallots, dill weed, salt and pepper. Toss to mix and serve warm.

MAKES 6 TO 8 SERVINGS

Green Bean, Tomato and Potato Salad

Dijon Balsamic Dressing

1/4	cup olive oil
5	tablespoons balsamic vinegar
1	tablespoon Dijon mustard
1/4	teaspoon salt
1/4	teaspoon pepper
1/3	cup chopped fresh basil
1/2	cup sliced green onions

Salad

12	ounces fresh green beans, trimmed and halved
1 3/4	pounds small red potatoes
2	teaspoons salt
1	pint grape tomatoes, halved

Dressing

Whisk the olive oil, balsamic vinegar, Dijon mustard, salt and pepper in a bowl. Stir in the basil and green onions.

Salad

Cook the beans in a saucepan of boiling water until tender-crisp; drain. Plunge the beans into ice water until cold; drain. Cover the potatoes with water in a saucepan and add the salt. Cook just until the potatoes are tender; drain. Cut the hot potatoes into bite-size pieces and place in a bowl. Add the dressing and toss to coat. Add the beans and mix gently. Chill for several hours. Let stand at room temperature for 1 hour before serving. Add the tomatoes and toss gently to mix.

MAKES 8 SERVINGS

Crustless Summer Squash Quiche

1	pound green or yellow summer squash	2	tablespoons chopped fresh herbs such as dill weed, basil, oregano or tarragon
4	eggs, well beaten	1½	teaspoons salt
2	cups (8 ounces) shredded Swiss cheese or Monterey Jack cheese	¼	cup (1 ounce) grated Parmesan cheese

Cook the squash and mash in a bowl, or grate the uncooked squash and squeeze out any excess moisture. Combine the squash, eggs, Swiss cheese, herbs and salt in a bowl and mix well. Spoon into a greased 8-inch baking dish and sprinkle with the Parmesan cheese. Bake at 350 degrees for 20 to 30 minutes or until the center is set and the edges are light brown.

MAKES 4 SERVINGS

Southern Squash Casserole

¼	cup water	1	cup milk
2	pounds yellow squash, sliced	1¾	cups (7 ounces) shredded sharp Cheddar cheese
1	onion, sliced	¼	cup fresh bread crumbs
1	teaspoon salt	2	tablespoons butter, melted
½	teaspoon pepper	¼	cup (1 ounce) shredded sharp Cheddar cheese
1	tablespoon butter, melted		
3	tablespoons all-purpose flour		
2	eggs, lightly beaten		

Combine the water, squash, onion and salt in a large saucepan and bring to a boil. Simmer, covered, for 20 minutes or until the squash is tender. Mash the squash and onion. Add the pepper, 1 tablespoon butter, the flour, eggs, and milk and mix well. Stir in 1¾ cups cheese. Spoon the mixture into a buttered 1½-quart casserole dish. Bake at 350 degrees for 30 minutes or until a knife inserted near the center comes out almost clean. Mix the bread crumbs and 2 tablespoons butter in a bowl and sprinkle over the squash. Sprinkle ¼ cup cheese over the top. Bake for 5 minutes longer or until the cheese is melted and the top is light brown.

MAKES 8 SERVINGS

Bentonville Farmers' Market Tomatoes

5   tomatoes, sliced
8   ounces fresh mozzarella cheese, sliced
1   red onion, thinly sliced
8   basil leaves, chopped
     Balsamic vinegar
     Salt and pepper to taste

Layer the tomatoes, cheese and onion in a fan shape on a serving platter. Sprinkle with the basil. Drizzle generously with the balsamic vinegar so that the tomatoes, cheese and onion are resting in vinegar. Let stand for at least 30 minutes. Season with salt and pepper and serve.

MAKES 6 SERVINGS

Town Square Tomatoes

2   garlic cloves
1   teaspoon salt
10 to 15 tomatoes, cut into cubes
2   tablespoons lemon juice
5   tablespoons dried mint
1/2   cup olive oil

Crush the garlic into the salt in a large bowl. Add the tomatoes, lemon juice and mint and mix well. Add the olive oil and mix well. Marinate for 3 to 4 hours before serving.

MAKES 8 TO 10 SERVINGS

Tomatoes Vinaigrette

6   tablespoons chopped fresh parsley
4   large tomatoes, chopped
1   garlic clove, crushed
6   tablespoons vegetable oil
2   tablespoons white vinegar
1   teaspoon salt
1/2   heaping teaspoon dried basil
1   teaspoon sugar
1/8   teaspoon pepper

Sprinkle the parsley over the tomatoes in a bowl. Whisk the garlic, oil, vinegar, salt, basil, sugar and pepper in a small bowl. Pour over the tomatoes and mix gently. Chill for 3 to 10 hours.

MAKES 8 SERVINGS

Fresh Salsa

4   tomatoes, peeled and chopped
1/3   cup minced onion
2   jalapeño chiles, seeded and minced
2   serrano chiles, seeded and minced
1   tablespoon olive oil
1   tablespoon red wine vinegar
1   teaspoon cumin
1   teaspoon salt
1   garlic clove, minced
1   tablespoon chopped cilantro

Combine the tomatoes, onion, jalapeño chiles, serrano chiles, olive oil, wine vinegar, cumin, salt, garlic and cilantro in a bowl and mix well. Let stand for 1 hour. Serve with your favorite chips.

MAKES 8 SERVINGS

Spinach-Stuffed Zucchini

6	zucchini, trimmed	1/2	cup (2 ounces) shredded
8	ounces frozen spinach, thawed		Cheddar cheese
	and well drained	2	slices bacon, crisp-cooked
4	ounces ricotta cheese		and crumbled
1	egg, beaten		Paprika
1/4	teaspoon nutmeg		

Cook the zucchini in a saucepan of boiling water for 8 to 10 minutes or until tender; drain. Cut the zucchini in half lengthwise. Scoop the pulp carefully onto a cutting board, leaving 1/4-inch shells. Chop the pulp finely and remove to a bowl. Add the spinach, ricotta cheese, egg and nutmeg and mix well. Spoon into the zucchini shells and sprinkle with the Cheddar cheese, bacon and paprika. Arrange the stuffed zucchini in a greased baking pan. Bake at 350 degrees for 15 to 20 minutes or until golden brown.

MAKES 8 TO 10 SERVINGS

Tomato Relish

24	ripe tomatoes, peeled	2	cups white vinegar
	and chopped	1	tablespoon salt
6	green bell peppers, chopped	2	teaspoons celery salt
8	onions, chopped	1/2	teaspoon cinnamon
6	hot chiles, seeded and chopped	1/4	teaspoon cloves
2 1/2	cups sugar	1/4	teaspoon allspice

Combine the tomatoes, bell peppers, onions, chiles, sugar, vinegar, salt, celery salt, cinnamon, cloves and allspice in a large stockpot. Bring to a boil, stirring frequently. Reduce the heat and simmer for 1 to 2 hours or to desired consistency, stirring occasionally. Ladle into hot canning jars, leaving 1/2-inch headspace; seal with 2-piece lids. Process in a boiling water bath for 20 minutes. Serve with ham, cold cuts, scrambled eggs or as a condiment.

MAKES 10 PINTS

Bread and Butter Pickles

4	quarts sliced pickling cucumbers (about 4 to 4 1/2 pounds)
6	white onions, thinly sliced
2	bell peppers, sliced
1/3	cup salt
1 1/2	teaspoons turmeric
1 1/2	teaspoons celery seeds
2	tablespoons mustard seeds
3	cups white vinegar
5	cups sugar

Combine the cucumbers, onions and bell peppers in a large stainless steel stockpot. Add the salt and mix well. Cover with ice and let stand for 3 hours; drain well. Combine the turmeric, celery seeds, mustard seeds, vinegar and sugar in a bowl and mix well. Add to the cucumber mixture and bring to a boil, stirring frequently. Ladle into hot canning jars, leaving 1/2-inch headspace; seal with 2-piece lids. Process in a boiling water bath for 10 minutes.

MAKES 10 PINTS

Fayetteville Farmers' Market Pesto

4	cups packed fresh basil leaves
4	garlic cloves
1/2	cup pine nuts
1	cup (4 ounces) grated Parmesan cheese
2	tablespoons fresh lemon juice
1/2 to 3/4	cup (or more) olive oil
	Kosher salt to taste

Combine the basil, garlic, pine nuts, cheese and lemon juice in a food processor and pulse a few times. Add the olive oil in a fine stream, processing constantly until of the desired consistency. Season with salt. Use immediately or spoon into small freezer containers and add a small amount of olive oil over the top. Freeze until ready to use.

MAKES 6 SERVINGS

Apple Orchard Cake

1¼   cups vegetable oil
2   cups sugar
3   eggs
3   cups all-purpose flour
½   teaspoon salt
1½   teaspoons baking soda
2   teaspoons vanilla extract
3   cups chopped peeled apples
1   cup chopped pecans, toasted

Beat the oil and sugar in a mixing bowl until light and fluffy. Add the eggs and beat for 2 minutes. Add the flour, salt, baking soda and vanilla and mix well. Fold in the apples and pecans. Pour into a greased and floured 9×13-inch baking pan. Bake at 325 degrees for 40 minutes. Increase the temperature to 350 degrees and bake for 15 minutes longer. Remove to a wire rack to cool. Cut into squares when cool.

MAKES 12 SERVINGS

Fresh Apple Muffins

½   cup all-purpose flour
¾   cup whole wheat flour
2   teaspoons baking powder
1   teaspoon salt
¾   teaspoon cinnamon
½   cup (1 stick) butter, melted
½   cup packed brown sugar
⅓   cup milk
1   egg, lightly beaten
1   cup shredded unpeeled apples

Sift the all-purpose flour, whole wheat flour, baking powder, salt and cinnamon into a bowl. Add the butter, brown sugar, milk, egg and apples and stir just until moistened. Fill greased muffin cups two-thirds full. Bake at 350 degrees for 30 minutes. Remove to a wire rack to cool.

MAKES 12 SERVINGS

Big Red Apple Shortcake

SHORTCAKE CRUST

1	cup sifted all-purpose flour
1/4	teaspoon salt
6	tablespoons shortening
2	tablespoons ice water

APPLE FILLING

6	large Rome apples, peeled and chopped
3/4	cup sugar
3	tablespoons water
1	tablespoon butter
1/4	teaspoon cinnamon

CRUST

Combine the flour and salt in a bowl. Cut in the shortening with a pastry blender or fork until crumbly. Add the ice water gradually and stir just until the mixture forms a dough. Roll out the dough thinly on a floured work surface and cut into twelve squares or circles. Prick the dough with a fork and arrange on an ungreased baking sheet. Bake at 400 degrees for 10 to 15 minutes or until light brown. Remove to a wire rack to cool.

FILLING

Combine the apples, sugar, water, butter and cinnamon in a saucepan. Simmer over medium heat until the apples are tender, stirring occasionally. Spoon equal portions of the filling over six baked crusts. Top with the remaining crusts. Serve with ice cream or whipped cream.

MAKES 6 SERVINGS

Apple Butter

8	cups cooked apple pulp
4	cups sugar
2	teaspoons cinnamon
1/4	teaspoon cloves

Combine the apple pulp, sugar, cinnamon and cloves in a large saucepan. Cook over medium heat for 15 minutes, stirring constantly. Ladle into hot canning jars, leaving 1/2-inch headspace; seal with 2-piece lids. Process in a boiling water bath for 10 minutes.

MAKES 5 PINTS

Apple Bread Pudding with Vanilla Sauce

PUDDING

1	loaf challah, cut into 16 (1/2-inch) slices
2	tablespoons butter
4	Golden Delicious, Gala or Granny Smith apples, peeled and cut into 1/4-inch slices
5	eggs
2/3	cup sugar
3	cups milk

1 1/2	teaspoons vanilla extract
1	tablespoon sugar
1	teaspoon cinnamon

VANILLA SAUCE

1/2	cup granulated sugar
1/2	cup packed brown sugar
1/2	cup heavy cream
1/2	cup (1 stick) butter, softened
1	teaspoon vanilla extract

PUDDING

Arrange the bread slices in the bottom of a greased 9×13-inch baking dish, overlapping the slices if necessary. Melt half the butter in a skillet. Add half the apples and cook for 2 1/2 minutes. Turn the apples over and cook for 2 1/2 minutes longer. Arrange over the bread in the baking dish. Repeat with the remaining butter and apples. Whisk the eggs, 2/3 cup sugar, the milk and vanilla in a bowl. Pour evenly over the apple layer. Mix 1 tablespoon sugar and the cinnamon in a small bowl and sprinkle over the layers. Bake at 325 degrees for 45 minutes or until a knife inserted in the center comes out clean. Remove to a wire rack.

SAUCE

Mix the granulated sugar, brown sugar, cream, butter and vanilla in a saucepan. Bring just to a boil, stirring frequently. Serve warm over the bread pudding.

MAKES 12 SERVINGS

> For a fall party, fill large glass storage jars with a mixture of apple cider, ginger ale, and ripe red apples that have been frozen overnight. Surround the jar with a ring of apples and serve with a ladle.

Farmers' markets are plentiful in Northwest Arkansas. They're at the downtown squares of Bentonville and Fayetteville, as well as the Jones Center in Springdale and Frisco Park in Rogers. Fresh-picked fruits, vegetables, herbs, and flowers are available from early spring to fall. All are limited to vendors with locally grown produce.

Sour Cream Blueberry Pie

1	cup sour cream	2 1/2	cups fresh blueberries
2	tablespoons	1	unbaked (9-inch) pie shell
	all-purpose flour	3	tablespoons unsalted butter,
3/4	cup sugar		softened
1	teaspoon vanilla extract	3	tablespoons chopped nuts
1/4	teaspoon salt	3	tablespoons
1	egg		all-purpose flour

Combine the sour cream, 2 tablespoons flour, the sugar, vanilla, salt and egg in a bowl and mix until smooth. Fold in the blueberries. Pour into the pie shell. Bake at 400 degrees for 25 minutes. Combine the butter, nuts and 3 tablespoons flour in a bowl and mix until crumbly. Sprinkle over the filling and bake for 10 minutes longer. Remove to a wire rack to cool.

MAKES 8 TO 10 SERVINGS

Blueberry Streusel Bread

BREAD

1/4	cup (1/2 stick) butter, softened	2	cups fresh blueberries or frozen blueberries, thawed
3/4	cup sugar		
1	egg		**STREUSEL TOPPING**
1/2	cup milk	1/2	cup sugar
2	cups all-purpose flour	1/3	cup all-purpose flour
2	teaspoons baking powder	1/2	teaspoon cinnamon
1/2	teaspoon salt	1/4	cup (1/2 stick) butter, cut into pieces

BREAD

Beat the butter and sugar in a mixing bowl until light and fluffy. Beat in the egg. Beat in the milk. Add the flour, baking powder and salt and stir just until combined. Fold in the blueberries. Spoon into a greased 9-inch baking dish.

TOPPING

Combine the sugar, flour and cinnamon in a bowl. Cut in the butter with a pastry blender or fork until crumbly. Sprinkle over the batter in the baking dish. Bake at 375 degrees for 45 minutes or until a wooden pick inserted in the center comes out clean. Remove to a wire rack to cool.

MAKES 9 SERVINGS

Blueberry Bread with Vanilla Sauce

BREAD

2	cups all-purpose flour
1	cup sugar
2 1/2	teaspoons baking powder
1/2	teaspoon salt
1	egg
1	cup milk
3	tablespoons vegetable oil
2	cups fresh blueberries or frozen blueberries, thawed

VANILLA SAUCE

1	cup sugar
1	tablespoon cornstarch
1	cup heavy cream
1/2	cup (1 stick) butter, cut into cubes

BREAD

Mix the flour, sugar, baking powder and salt together. Beat the egg, milk and oil in a mixing bowl. Add the dry ingredients and beat just until combined. Fold in the blueberries. Pour into a greased 5×9-inch loaf pan. Bake at 350 degrees for 50 to 55 minutes or until a wooden pick inserted in the center comes out clean. Cool in the pan for 10 minutes. Remove to a wire rack to cool completely.

SAUCE

Combine the sugar and cornstarch in a saucepan. Add the cream and stir until smooth. Add the butter. Bring to a boil over medium heat, stirring frequently. Cook for 2 minutes or until thickened, stirring constantly. Serve with the bread.

MAKES 8 SERVINGS

COMFORT FOOD

TLC for Family
and Friends

Potato Lasagna

1½   *pounds ground beef*
1½   *cups chopped onions*
2   *garlic cloves, minced*
1   *(32-ounce) jar spaghetti sauce*
⅓   *cup water*
1½   *teaspoons salt*
1   *teaspoon dried basil*
1   *teaspoon dried oregano*
1   *teaspoon sugar*
¼   *teaspoon pepper*
5   *potatoes, peeled and thinly sliced*
2   *cups (8 ounces) shredded mozzarella cheese*

Brown the ground beef with the onions and garlic in a skillet, stirring until the ground beef is crumbly; drain. Add the spaghetti sauce, water, salt, basil, oregano, sugar and pepper and mix well. Cook over medium heat for 2 minutes, stirring frequently. Spread one-third of the meat sauce over the bottom of a 9×13-inch baking dish. Arrange half the potatoes over the top. Spread half the remaining meat sauce over the potatoes and arrange the remaining potatoes over the meat sauce. Spread the remaining meat sauce over the top. Cover tightly with foil. Bake at 375 degrees for 55 to 60 minutes. Remove the foil. Sprinkle with the cheese and bake until the cheese is melted. Remove to a wire rack and let stand for 10 minutes before serving.

MAKES 10 TO 12 SERVINGS

Baked Lasagna

1½ pounds ground beef
1   garlic clove, minced
1   tablespoon parsley flakes
1   tablespoon basil
1½ teaspoons salt
1   (16-ounce) can diced tomatoes
1   (6-ounce) can tomato paste
3   cups cream-style cottage cheese
2   eggs, beaten
2   teaspoons salt
2   tablespoons parsley flakes
½   cup (2 ounces) grated Parmesan cheese
10 ounces lasagna noodles, cooked al dente, drained and rinsed
16 ounces mozzarella cheese, shredded

Brown the ground beef in a skillet, stirring until crumbly; drain. Add the garlic, 1 tablespoon parsley flakes, the basil, 1½ teaspoons salt, the tomatoes and tomato paste and mix well. Simmer for 30 minutes, stirring occasionally. Combine the cottage cheese, eggs, 2 teaspoons salt, 2 tablespoons parsley flakes and Parmesan cheese in a bowl and mix well. Arrange half the noodles in the bottom of a 9×13-inch baking dish and spread with half the cottage cheese mixture. Sprinkle with half the mozzarella cheese and top with half the meat sauce. Repeat the layers to use the remaining noodles, cottage cheese mixture, mozzarella cheese and meat sauce. Bake at 375 degrees for 30 minutes.

MAKES 12 SERVINGS

Baked Spaghetti

1	pound ground beef
1	(26-ounce) jar spaghetti sauce
16	ounces spaghetti, cooked al dente and drained
8	ounces cream cheese, cut into thin slices
2	cups (8 ounces) shredded mozzarella, Cheddar or Italian-style mixed cheese

Brown the ground beef in a skillet, stirring until crumbly; drain. Stir in the spaghetti sauce and simmer for 5 minutes. Spread the cooked pasta over the bottom of a greased 9×13-inch baking dish. Arrange the cream cheese over the pasta. Spoon the meat sauce over the top. Sprinkle with the mozzarella cheese. Bake at 350 degrees for 30 minutes or until bubbly.

MAKES 8 TO 10 SERVINGS

> No need to spend a fortune on a new tablecloth. Simply purchase a piece of fabric and create a no-sew hem with an iron and fusible interfacing. For an extra touch, glue cut flower heads to a fabric square for a beautiful table topper.

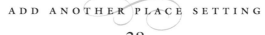

Cheesy Beefy Noodle Casserole

2	pounds ground beef
2	teaspoons salt
1	teaspoon garlic salt
1	teaspoon Italian seasoning
2	teaspoons sugar
	Pepper to taste
4	(8-ounce) cans tomato sauce
8	ounces cream cheese, softened
1	cup sour cream
5	green onions, thinly sliced
12	ounces egg noodles, cooked and drained
2	cups (8 ounces) shredded Cheddar cheese

Brown the ground beef in a skillet, stirring until crumbly; drain. Add the salt, garlic salt, Italian seasoning, sugar and pepper and mix well. Stir in the tomato sauce and simmer for 15 minutes. Combine the cream cheese, sour cream and green onions in a bowl and mix well. Spread half the noodles over the bottom of a buttered 10×15-inch baking dish. Spread half the meat sauce over the noodles. Top evenly with half the cream cheese mixture and sprinkle with half the Cheddar cheese. Repeat the layers to use the remaining noodles, meat sauce, cream cheese mixture and Cheddar cheese. Bake at 350 degrees for 30 minutes.

MAKES 6 TO 8 SERVINGS

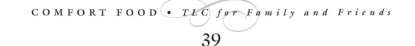

Chicken Imperial

2	cups bread crumbs
1/4	cup fresh parsley, minced
1	garlic clove, minced
1 1/2	teaspoons salt
	Pepper to taste
1	cup (2 sticks) butter, melted
1	tablespoon Dijon mustard
1	teaspoon Worcestershire sauce
8	boneless chicken breasts or chicken thighs
	Parsley sprigs for garnish

Combine the bread crumbs, minced parsley, garlic, salt and pepper in a shallow dish and mix well. Combine the butter, Dijon mustard and Worcestershire sauce in a bowl and mix well. Coat the chicken in the butter mixture and then press into the bread crumbs, coating all sides. Arrange the chicken in a greased 9×13-inch baking dish. Drizzle any remaining butter mixture over the top. Bake at 350 degrees for 1 hour or until the chicken is cooked through. Garnish with parsley sprigs.

MAKES 8 SERVINGS

Poppy Seed Chicken

5 or	6 boneless chicken breasts, cooked and cut into bite-size pieces
1	cup sour cream
1	(10-ounce) can condensed cream of chicken soup
1	tablespoon poppy seeds
1	sleeve butter crackers, crushed
1/2	cup (1 stick) butter, melted

Combine the chicken, sour cream, soup and poppy seeds in a bowl and mix well. Spoon into a 9×13-inch baking dish. Sprinkle the crackers over the chicken mixture. Drizzle the butter over the top. Bake at 350 degrees for 30 minutes or until bubbly.

MAKES 8 TO 10 SERVINGS

Artichoke and Chicken Casserole

1	garlic clove, chopped
1	onion, chopped
8	ounces sliced button mushrooms
3	tablespoons butter
1	(10-ounce) can condensed cream of mushroom soup
1/2	cup mayonnaise
1	teaspoon Worcestershire sauce
2	tablespoons sherry
1	cup (4 ounces) shredded Cheddar cheese
	Salt and pepper to taste
1	(10-ounce) package frozen chopped spinach, thawed and well drained
1	(14-ounce) can artichoke hearts, drained and cut into quarters
6	boneless chicken breasts, cooked and cut into bite-size pieces
1/2	cup (2 ounces) grated Parmesan cheese

Sauté the garlic, onion and mushrooms in the butter in a skillet until tender. Add the soup, mayonnaise, Worcestershire sauce, sherry, Cheddar cheese, salt and pepper and mix well. Stir in the spinach. Spread the artichokes over the bottom of a buttered 9×13-inch baking dish and top with the chicken. Pour the spinach mixture over the chicken and sprinkle with the Parmesan cheese. Bake at 375 degrees for 20 minutes or until bubbly.

MAKES 8 TO 10 SERVINGS

Parmesan Chicken

1	cup bread crumbs
1/2	cup plus 2 tablespoons grated Parmesan cheese
1 1/2	tablespoons minced fresh parsley, or 3/4 teaspoon parsley flakes
1/2	teaspoon salt
1/4	teaspoon pepper
1/4	cup (or more) milk
6 to	8 boneless skinless chicken breasts
1/4	cup (1/2 stick) butter, melted
1/4	teaspoon garlic powder
	Juice of 1 lemon
	Dash of paprika

Combine the bread crumbs, cheese, parsley, salt and pepper in a shallow dish and mix well. Pour the milk into a shallow dish. Coat the chicken in the milk and then press into the bread crumb mixture, coating all sides. Arrange the chicken in a lightly greased 9×13-inch baking dish. Combine the butter, garlic powder and lemon juice in a bowl and mix well. Drizzle over the chicken and sprinkle with paprika. Bake at 350 degrees for 45 to 55 minutes or until bubbly and the chicken is cooked through.

MAKES 6 TO 8 SERVINGS

Fill ordinary glass vases with buttons,
citrus, nuts, or other small items for a unique anchor
for a casual flower arrangement.

Chicken and Wild Rice Casserole

This casserole can be frozen for up to one month. Double the baking time if baked frozen.

2	(6-ounce) packages long grain and wild rice mix
3¼	cups canned chicken broth
1	cup dry sherry
½	cup (1 stick) butter
16	ounces mushrooms, sliced
1	cup chopped green onions
2	chickens, cooked, boned and chopped or shredded
1	cup sour cream
1	(10-ounce) can condensed cream of mushroom soup
1	sleeve butter crackers, crushed (about 1½ cups)
1	(6-ounce) can French-fried onions
¼	cup (½ stick) butter, melted
¼	teaspoon paprika
⅛	teaspoon garlic powder

Cook the rice mix according to the package directions, substituting the broth and sherry for water and omitting the butter. Melt ½ cup butter in a skillet. Add the mushrooms and green onions and sauté for 10 minutes or until tender. Stir in the chicken, sour cream, soup and rice and cook until heated through. Spoon into a 10×15-inch baking dish or three 8×8-inch baking dishes. Mix the crushed crackers and French-fried onions in a bowl. Add ¼ cup butter, the paprika and garlic powder and mix well. Drizzle evenly over the chicken mixture. Bake, covered, at 350 degrees for 25 to 30 minutes. Bake, uncovered, for 5 to 10 minutes longer or until bubbly.

MAKES 10 TO 12 SERVINGS

Homecoming Chicken Casserole

1   (6-ounce) package long grain and wild rice mix
1½   cups water
1   (10-ounce) can condensed cream of celery soup
1   (10-ounce) can condensed cream of chicken soup
1   (6-ounce) can sliced water chestnuts, drained
1   (6-ounce) jar chopped pimentos
6   boneless chicken breasts
2   tablespoons butter, softened
        Salt and pepper to taste

Combine the rice mix, water, celery soup, chicken soup, water chestnuts and pimentos in a bowl and mix well. Spoon evenly into a 9×13-inch baking dish. Arrange the chicken on top. Spread the butter over the chicken and season with salt and pepper. Bake at 250 degrees for 2½ hours.

MAKES 6 SERVINGS

Chicken Stuffing Casserole

3   packages herb-seasoned stuffing mix with
        seasoning packets
3/4   cup (1½ sticks) butter, melted
2   cups water
2   boneless skinless chicken breasts, cooked and
        cut into bite-size pieces
1   (10-ounce) can condensed cream of chicken soup
3   cups sour cream

Combine the stuffing mix, butter and water in a bowl and mix well. Spread half the stuffing mixture over the bottom of a lightly buttered 9×13-inch baking dish and top evenly with the chicken. Combine the soup and sour cream in a bowl and mix well. Spread over the chicken and top with the remaining stuffing mixture. Bake at 350 degrees for 45 minutes.

MAKES 10 TO 12 SERVINGS

Country Chicken Potpie

1   *(32-ounce) bag frozen mixed vegetables, thawed*
4   *cups cubed cooked chicken*
1   *(10-ounce) can condensed cream of chicken soup*
1   *(10-ounce) can condensed chicken broth*
1/2   *teaspoon dried tarragon*
1 1/2   *cups all-purpose flour*
2   *teaspoons baking powder*
1 1/2   *cups buttermilk*
1/2   *cup (1 stick) butter, melted*

Combine the vegetables, chicken, soup, broth and tarragon in a bowl and mix well. Spoon into a greased 9×13-inch baking pan. Mix the flour and baking powder in a bowl. Add the buttermilk and butter and stir to form a thin dough. Pour the dough evenly over the chicken mixture. Bake at 350 degrees for 1 hour or until the top is light brown.

MAKES 6 TO 8 SERVINGS

Excellent Enchiladas

4   boneless skinless chicken breasts,
      boiled and shredded
6   ounces fresh spinach, trimmed and
      torn into bite-size pieces
2   cups chopped button mushrooms
1   tablespoon minced garlic
2   jalapeño chiles, seeded and minced
1   (4-ounce) can chopped green chiles
4   cups (16 ounces) shredded Monterey Jack cheese
2   cups sour cream
3/4   (15-ounce) can pinto beans, drained
3/4   (15-ounce) can black beans, drained
2   bunches green onions, chopped
1   (2-ounce) can sliced black olives, drained
1   (17-ounce) jar mild enchilada sauce
12 to 16 flour tortillas

Combine the chicken, spinach, mushrooms, garlic, jalapeño chiles, green chiles, cheese, sour cream, pinto beans, black beans, half the green onions and half the olives in a bowl and mix well. Pour 1/2 cup of the enchilada sauce onto a plate. Coat both sides of the tortillas in the enchilada sauce and remove to a work surface. Spoon equal portions of the chicken mixture onto the tortillas. Roll up the tortillas and secure with wooden picks. Arrange the enchiladas in a 9×13-inch baking pan. Pour the remaining enchilada sauce evenly over the top and sprinkle with the remaining green onions and olives. Bake at 350 degrees for 20 to 25 minutes.

MAKES 6 TO 8 SERVINGS

Ham and Hash Brown Take-Along

1   (32-ounce) package frozen shredded
    hash brown potatoes, slightly thawed
8   ounces diced cooked ham
2   (10-ounce) cans condensed cream of potato soup
2   cups sour cream
2   cups (8 ounces) shredded sharp Cheddar cheese
1   cup (4 ounces) grated Parmesan cheese

Combine the potatoes, ham, soup, sour cream and Cheddar cheese in a bowl and mix well. Spoon into a greased 9×13-inch baking dish and sprinkle with the Parmesan cheese. Bake at 350 degrees for 1 hour or until bubbly and light brown.

MAKES 12 TO 16 SERVINGS

Fayetteville is the first home of President Bill and U.S. Senator Hillary Clinton. Both taught at the University of Arkansas School of Law. They were married in 1975 in the living room of their home, which is now the Clinton House Museum. Displays include memorabilia of President Clinton's blossoming political career, including some of his early political speeches. The museum is open to the public.

Homemade Chicken Noodle Soup

1	chicken
3	ribs celery
3	chicken bouillon cubes
2	ribs celery, chopped
3	carrots, chopped
1	(16-ounce) can condensed cream of chicken soup
1	tablespoon oregano
24	ounces egg noodles
	Salt and pepper to taste

Place the chicken and 3 ribs celery in a stockpot and add enough water to cover the chicken. Bring to a boil and reduce the heat. Simmer for 1 hour or until the chicken is cooked through. Remove the celery with a slotted spoon and discard. Remove the chicken to a work surface and let cool, reserving the cooking liquid. Chop the chicken, discarding the skin and bones. Add the chicken, bouillon cubes, 2 ribs celery, the carrots, soup, oregano, noodles, salt and pepper to the cooking liquid. Bring to a boil, stirring occasionally. Reduce the heat and simmer for 20 minutes.

MAKES 10 TO 12 SERVINGS

Tortellini Soup

2	tablespoons olive oil
1	yellow onion, chopped
3	garlic cloves, minced
1	(15-ounce) can chopped tomatoes
8	cups chicken broth
1	chicken, cooked, boned and cut into bite-size pieces
1/4	cup pesto
1	(9-ounce) package refrigerator cheese tortellini
16	ounces fresh spinach, rinsed, trimmed and chopped
	Salt and pepper to taste

Heat the olive oil in a large saucepan over medium heat. Add the onion and sauté for 10 minutes or until tender. Add the garlic and tomatoes and sauté for 10 minutes. Add the broth and bring to a boil. Add the chicken and reduce the heat to low. Stir in the pesto and tortellini and simmer for 5 minutes. Add the spinach and simmer for 5 minutes. Season with salt and pepper and serve.

MAKES 10 SERVINGS

Turn seasonal produce into a centerpiece. Use apples, artichokes, pomegranates, or citrus in floral arrangements for extra impact. Toss in fragrant herbs, such as mint, rosemary, and sage, to add extra texture and scent.

Vegetarian Chili

1	onion, chopped
1	green bell pepper, chopped
2	teaspoons vegetable oil
1	(28-ounce) can crushed tomatoes
1	(15-ounce) can dark red kidney beans, drained and rinsed
1	(15-ounce) can chili beans
1	(15-ounce) can whole kernel corn
1	(6-ounce) can tomato paste
1	(4-ounce) can whole green chiles
1/4	cup chili powder
1	tablespoon cumin
1	teaspoon salt
1/2	teaspoon pepper
6 to	8 teaspoons sour cream
6 to	8 tablespoons shredded Cheddar cheese

Sauté the onion and bell pepper in the oil in a large saucepan until tender. Stir in the tomatoes, kidney beans, chili beans, corn, tomato paste, green chiles, chili powder, cumin, salt and pepper. Bring to a boil, stirring frequently. Reduce the heat and simmer for 1 hour. Ladle into serving bowls and top each with 1 teaspoon of the sour cream and 1 tablespoon of the cheese.

MAKES 6 TO 8 SERVINGS

White Chili

1/4	cup (1/2 stick) butter
2	large white onions, chopped
1	jalapeño chile, chopped
1/3	cup all-purpose flour
4	cups chicken broth
3	cups half-and-half
3	(15-ounce) cans Great Northern beans, drained and rinsed
2 or 3	(4-ounce) cans chopped green chiles
4	cups chopped cooked chicken breasts
2	teaspoons salt
1/2	teaspoon white pepper
1	tablespoon chili powder
1	tablespoon cumin
1	tablespoon hot red pepper sauce
1 1/2	cups (6 ounces) shredded Monterey Jack cheese
1	cup sour cream
	Avocado slices and lime wedges for garnish

Melt the butter in a large saucepan over medium heat. Add the onions and jalapeño chile and sauté until tender. Add the flour and cook for 5 minutes, stirring frequently. Whisk in the chicken broth and half-and-half gradually. Simmer for 10 minutes or until thickened, stirring frequently. Stir in the beans, green chiles, chicken, salt, white pepper, chili powder, cumin and hot sauce. Simmer for 20 minutes, stirring occasionally. Stir in the cheese and sour cream. Cook just until the cheese is melted, stirring constantly. Ladle into soup bowls and garnish with avocado slices and lime wedges.

MAKES 6 TO 8 SERVINGS

Home-Style Corn Casserole

1	(15-ounce) can whole kernel corn, drained	1/2	cup water	
1	(15-ounce) can cream-style corn	1	cup corn muffin mix	
2	eggs, beaten	1/4	cup (1/2 stick) butter, melted	
1	small onion, chopped	1	cup (4 ounces) shredded sharp Cheddar cheese	

Combine the whole kernel corn, cream-style corn, eggs, onion, water, muffin mix and butter in a bowl and mix well. Spoon into a 7×11-inch baking dish. Bake at 350 degrees for 55 minutes. Sprinkle with the cheese and bake for 5 minutes longer.

MAKES 8 TO 10 SERVINGS

PHOTO ON PAGE 35

Party Potatoes

8 to	10 russet potatoes, peeled	12	ounces Cheddar cheese, shredded	
1	cup sour cream			
8	ounces cream cheese, softened	6 to	8 slices bacon, crisp-cooked and crumbled	
1/4	cup (1/2 stick) butter			
	Salt and pepper to taste	2	cups sliced green onions	

Cover the potatoes with water in a saucepan. Bring to a boil and cook until tender; drain. Combine the sour cream and cream cheese in a large bowl and mix well. Add the hot potatoes and mash until smooth. Add the butter, salt and pepper and stir until the butter is melted. Spoon into a well greased 9×13-inch baking dish and sprinkle with the cheese, bacon and green onions. Bake at 350 degrees for 25 minutes.

MAKES 8 TO 10 SERVINGS

Saturday Morning Chocolate Gravy

1/4   *cup baking cocoa*
1/4   *cup sugar*
1/4   *cup all-purpose flour*
2   *cups milk*
1   *egg, beaten*
1   *teaspoon vanilla extract*

Mix the baking cocoa, sugar and flour together. Combine the milk and egg in a saucepan. Bring to just below boiling, stirring constantly. Whisk in the dry ingredients. Cook until thickened, stirring constantly. Stir in the vanilla. Serve over biscuits.

MAKES 4 TO 6 SERVINGS

Shortcut Cinnamon Rolls

1   *(2-layer) package butter recipe yellow cake mix*
2   *envelopes dry yeast*
5   *cups all-purpose flour*
2 1/2   *cups hot water (not boiling)*
1/2   *cup (1 stick) butter, softened*
1   *cup granulated sugar*
1/4   *cup cinnamon*
2   *cups confectioners' sugar*
1/2   *cup milk*
2   *teaspoons vanilla extract*

Combine the cake mix, yeast and flour in a large bowl and mix well. Add the water and mix well. Cover and let rise in a warm place for 1 hour or until doubled in bulk. Divide the dough in half and roll out half the dough on a floured work surface to a large rectangle. Spread with half the butter. Mix the granulated sugar and cinnamon in a bowl. Sprinkle half over the buttered dough. Roll up the dough from the long side and cut into fifteen slices. Arrange the slices in a nonstick 9×13-inch baking pan. Repeat with the remaining dough, butter and cinnamon mixture and arrange in another nonstick 9×13-inch baking pan. Cover both pans and let rise in a warm place for 30 minutes or until doubled in bulk. Bake at 375 degrees for 20 to 25 minutes or until golden brown. Combine the confectioners' sugar, milk and vanilla in a bowl and mix until smooth. Drizzle over the warm rolls and serve.

MAKES 30 ROLLS

Bernice Jones's Chocolate Cherry Cake

1   (2-layer) package chocolate cake mix with pudding
1   (21-ounce) can cherry pie filling
2   eggs
1   teaspoon almond extract
1   cup sugar
1/3   cup milk
5   tablespoons butter
1   cup (6 ounces) chocolate chips

Combine the cake mix, pie filling, eggs, and almond extract in a bowl and mix well. Pour into a greased and floured 9×13-inch cake pan. Bake at 350 degrees for 30 to 40 minutes or until the cake tests done. Remove to a wire rack to cool. Combine the sugar, milk and butter in a saucepan. Bring to a boil, stirring frequently. Add the chocolate chips and cook until the chocolate is melted, stirring constantly. Pour over the cake and let cool before cutting.

MAKES 15 SERVINGS

The Jones Truck Line legacy is one of service and giving. Harvey Jones was successful in establishing and running one of the largest trucking businesses in the country. In his success he wanted to improve his community and the lives of his neighbors.
In 1938 he married Bernice Young, who was equally caring, giving, and supportive of the community. The Joneses were instrumental in the development of what is now Northwest Medical Center in Springdale. Their giving had a positive impact on many charities throughout the state, but the Jones Center for Families has been their legacy gift.

Triple-Layer Strawberry Dessert

2½   *cups finely crushed pretzels*
4½   *tablespoons sugar*
3/4   *cup (1½ sticks) butter, melted*
1   *cup sugar*
16   *ounces cream cheese, softened*
8   *ounces whipped topping*
1   *(3-ounce) package strawberry gelatin*
1   *cup boiling water*
32   *ounces frozen strawberries*

Combine the crushed pretzels, 4½ tablespoons sugar and the butter in a bowl and mix well. Press into the bottom of a 9×13-inch baking dish. Bake at 350 degrees for 10 minutes; do not overbake. Remove to a wire rack to cool completely. Beat 1 cup sugar and the cream cheese in a mixing bowl until smooth. Fold in the whipped topping. Spread evenly over the cooled crust. Chill for 30 minutes or until set. Combine the gelatin and boiling water in a heatproof bowl and stir until the gelatin is dissolved. Add the frozen strawberries and stir until the strawberries are thawed. Pour carefully over the cream cheese layer. Chill for 1 hour or until the gelatin is set.

MAKES 10 TO 12 SERVINGS

BREAD AND BREAKFAST

Sweet and Yeast Breads,
Breakfast Casseroles

Fiery Breakfast Casserole

1	pound hot pork sausage
6	slices bread, buttered
6	eggs
2	cups half-and-half
1	teaspoon salt
	Pepper to taste
	Dash of Worcestershire sauce
1	teaspoon dry mustard
16	ounces Cheddar cheese, shredded

Brown the sausage in a skillet, stirring until crumbly; drain. Toast the bread lightly and remove the crusts. Cut the bread into cubes and spread over the bottom of a buttered 9×13-inch baking dish. Spread the sausage evenly over the bread. Beat the eggs and half-and-half in a bowl lightly with a fork. Stir in the salt, pepper, Worcestershire sauce and dry mustard. Pour over the sausage layer. Sprinkle with the cheese. Chill, covered, overnight. Bake, uncovered, at 350 degrees for 35 to 40 minutes or until golden brown.

MAKES 12 SERVINGS

> Thanksgiving, Christmas, Easter, family gatherings, children's sleepovers, houseguests: a breakfast casserole prepared the night before is an easy way to treat your family and guests. You can sleep later knowing all you have to do is move a dish from the refrigerator to the oven. You'll wake to a clean kitchen and a delicious home-cooked meal.

Green Chile Strata

1	pound pork sausage
6	taco-size flour tortillas
2	(4-ounce) cans chopped green chiles, drained
4	cups (16 ounces) shredded Monterey Jack cheese and/or Cheddar cheese
5	eggs, beaten
2	cups milk
1	teaspoon salt
1	teaspoon paprika
1/2	teaspoon oregano
1/2	teaspoon garlic powder
1/2	teaspoon dry mustard

Brown the sausage in a skillet, stirring until crumbly; drain. Cut the tortillas into large strips and arrange half the strips over the bottom of a buttered 9×13-inch baking pan. Sprinkle with half the green chiles and half the cheese. Top evenly with the sausage. Repeat the layers to use the remaining tortilla strips, green chiles and cheese. Combine the eggs, milk, salt, paprika, oregano, garlic powder and dry mustard in a bowl and mix well. Pour over the layers in the baking pan. Chill, covered, for 30 minutes to overnight. Bake, uncovered, at 350 degrees for 30 to 35 minutes or until slightly puffed and bubbly. Let stand for 5 minutes before cutting into squares.

MAKES 15 SERVINGS

Ham Broccoli Strata

12	eggs
3 1/2	cups milk
2	tablespoons minced onion
1/4	teaspoon dry mustard
1/2	teaspoon salt
12	slices sandwich bread, torn into 1/2- to 3/4-inch pieces
12	ounces Cheddar cheese, shredded
1	(8-ounce) package frozen chopped broccoli, cooked and drained
1	cup chopped cooked ham

Beat the eggs in a large mixing bowl. Beat in the milk, onion, dry mustard and salt. Stir in the bread, cheese, broccoli and ham. Pour into a greased 9×13-inch baking pan. Chill, covered, for 6 hours to overnight. Bake, uncovered, at 325 degrees for 50 to 60 minutes or until set. Let stand for 10 minutes before serving.

MAKES 12 SERVINGS

Crustless Sausage Quiche

1	pound pork sausage
12	eggs
4	cups (16 ounces) shredded Cheddar cheese
1	tablespoon dry mustard
1/2	teaspoon Worcestershire sauce
1/2	cup milk
	Salt to taste

Brown the sausage in a skillet, stirring until crumbly; drain. Beat the eggs in a bowl. Add the sausage, cheese, dry mustard, Worcestershire sauce, milk and salt and mix well. Pour into a nonstick 9×13-inch baking pan. Bake at 350 degrees for 30 to 40 minutes or until set.

MAKES 12 SERVINGS

Bacon and Asparagus Quiche

8	ounces fresh asparagus, trimmed and cut into 1/2-inch pieces
1	unbaked (8-inch) pie shell
1	egg white, lightly beaten
5	slices bacon, crisp-cooked and crumbled
1	cup (4 ounces) shredded Swiss cheese
1/2	cup mushrooms, sliced
2	eggs
3/4	cup half-and-half
1/8	teaspoon nutmeg
	Salt and pepper to taste

Place the asparagus in a steamer rack over 1 inch of boiling water in a saucepan. Cook, covered, for 2 to 6 minutes or until tender-crisp. Remove the asparagus from the steamer rack and let cool. Brush the pie shell with the egg white. Sprinkle the asparagus and bacon into the pie shell. Top with the cheese and mushrooms. Beat the eggs, half-and-half, nutmeg, salt and pepper in a bowl and pour into the pie shell. Bake at 400 degrees for 35 to 40 minutes or until set. Remove to a wire rack and let cool before serving.

MAKES 6 SERVINGS

Spicy Cheese Grits

1	cup grits
1/2	cup (1 stick) butter
1	tablespoon Worcestershire sauce
1/2	teaspoon garlic salt
	Tabasco sauce to taste
12	ounces sharp Cheddar cheese, shredded
2	egg whites

Prepare the grits according to the package directions. Stir in the butter, Worcestershire sauce, garlic salt, Tabasco sauce and cheese. Beat the egg whites in a bowl until stiff. Fold gently into the grits mixture. Spoon into a buttered 2-quart baking dish. Bake at 350 degrees for 30 to 40 minutes or until set. Let stand for 5 minutes before serving.

MAKES 6 SERVINGS

Cheese Blintz Casserole

2	cups cottage cheese, drained
8	ounces cream cheese, softened
2	egg yolks
1	tablespoon sugar
1	teaspoon vanilla extract
1½	cups sour cream
½	cup orange juice
6	eggs
¼	cup (½ stick) butter, softened
1	cup all-purpose flour
⅓	cup sugar
2	teaspoons baking powder
½	teaspoon cinnamon
16	tablespoons fruit preserves
16	teaspoons sour cream

Beat the cottage cheese, cream cheese, egg yolks, 1 tablespoon sugar and the vanilla in a mixing bowl. Process 1½ cups sour cream, the orange juice, eggs and butter in a blender. Add the flour, ⅓ cup sugar, the baking powder and cinnamon and process until smooth. Pour half the sour cream mixture evenly into a greased 9×13-inch baking dish. Spread the cottage cheese mixture carefully over the top; it will mix slightly. Pour the remaining sour cream mixture over the cottage cheese mixture. Chill, covered, overnight. Bake, uncovered, at 350 degrees for 50 to 60 minutes or until slightly puffed and golden brown. Remove to a wire rack to cool. Cut into sixteen squares and top each square with 1 tablespoon of the fruit preserves and 1 teaspoon of the sour cream.

MAKES 16 SERVINGS

Cranberry French Toast

8	ounces cream cheese, softened
1/4	cup sugar
2	teaspoons vanilla extract
1	teaspoon cinnamon
4	eggs
2 1/2	cups milk
1	(24-inch) loaf French bread
1	cup fresh cranberries or frozen cranberries, thawed

Beat the cream cheese, sugar, vanilla and cinnamon at medium speed in a mixing bowl. Add the eggs one at a time, beating well after each addition. Beat in the milk gradually. Trim the ends from the bread and cut the loaf into 1-inch slices. Arrange the bread slices in a greased 9×13-inch baking dish and sprinkle with the cranberries. Pour the cream cheese mixture evenly over the top. Let stand for 15 minutes or chill overnight. Bake at 350 degrees for 40 to 45 minutes or until golden brown. Serve with Cranberry Syrup.

MAKES 8 SERVINGS

PHOTO ON PAGE 57

Cranberry Syrup

1	cup maple-flavored pancake syrup
1	cup fresh cranberries or frozen cranberries, thawed
2	tablespoons sugar

Bring the syrup just to boiling in a saucepan over medium heat. Stir in the cranberries and sugar and reduce the heat to low. Simmer for 10 minutes, stirring occasionally. Let cool slightly before serving.

MAKES 2 CUPS

Praline French Toast

FRENCH TOAST

1	loaf French bread, cut into 1-inch slices
8	eggs
2	cups half-and-half
1	cup milk
2	tablespoons sugar
1	teaspoon vanilla extract
1/4	teaspoon cinnamon
1/4	teaspoon nutmeg
	Dash of salt

PRALINE TOPPING AND ASSEMBLY

1	cup (2 sticks) butter, softened
1	cup packed light brown sugar
1	cup chopped pecans
2	tablespoons light corn syrup
1/2	teaspoon cinnamon
1/2	teaspoon nutmeg

FRENCH TOAST

Arrange the bread slices in two overlapping rows in a generously buttered 9×13-inch baking dish. Combine the eggs, half-and-half, milk, sugar, vanilla, cinnamon, nutmeg and salt in a bowl. Beat with a rotary beater or whisk until well mixed but not frothy. Pour evenly over the bread slices, making sure all of the bread is covered with the egg mixture. Chill, covered, overnight.

TOPPING

Combine the butter, brown sugar, pecans, corn syrup, cinnamon and nutmeg in a bowl and mix well. Spread evenly over the chilled bread in the baking dish. Bake, uncovered, at 350 degrees for 40 to 45 minutes or until puffed and golden brown. Serve with maple syrup.

MAKES 8 SERVINGS

Cinnamon Streusel Coffee Cake

2	cups all-purpose flour	1	cup buttermilk
1	teaspoon baking powder	3/4	cup (1 1/2 sticks) butter,
1	teaspoon baking soda		softened
1	teaspoon cinnamon	2	eggs, lightly beaten
1/2	teaspoon salt	1/2	cup packed brown sugar
3/4	cup granulated sugar	1	teaspoon cinnamon
1/2	cup packed brown sugar	1/2	cup chopped pecans (optional)

Combine the flour, baking powder, baking soda, 1 teaspoon cinnamon, the salt, granulated sugar, 1/2 cup brown sugar, the buttermilk, butter and eggs in a bowl and mix well. Pour into a greased 9×13-inch baking pan. Cover with plastic wrap and chill for 8 hours to overnight. Combine 1/2 cup brown sugar, 1 teaspoon cinnamon and the pecans in a bowl and mix well. Sprinkle evenly over the batter. Bake at 350 degrees for 30 to 35 minutes or until a wooden pick inserted in the center comes out clean. Remove to a wire rack to cool.

MAKES 12 SERVINGS

Refrigerator Muffins

1	(15-ounce) box bran cereal	2	teaspoons salt
	with raisins	4	eggs, beaten
5	cups all-purpose flour	4	cups buttermilk
3	cups sugar	1	cup vegetable oil
5	teaspoons baking soda	1/2	cup raisins

Combine the cereal, flour, sugar, baking soda and salt in a large bowl and mix well. Combine the eggs, buttermilk and oil in a bowl and mix well. Add to the cereal mixture and mix well. Fold in the raisins. Remove the batter to a tightly covered container and store in the refrigerator for up to 6 weeks, baking muffins as needed. Fill nonstick muffin cups two-thirds full. Bake at 400 degrees for 15 minutes. Remove to a wire rack to cool. You may add grated carrots, chopped nuts or sweetened dried cranberries to the batter just before baking.

MAKES 36

Cappuccino Muffins with Espresso Topping

MUFFINS

2   cups all-purpose flour
3/4   cup sugar
2 1/2   teaspoons baking powder
1   teaspoon cinnamon
1/2   teaspoon salt
2   tablespoons instant coffee granules
1   cup milk
1/2   cup (1 stick) butter, melted
1   egg, beaten
1   teaspoon vanilla extract
3/4   cup miniature semisweet chocolate chips

ESPRESSO TOPPING

4   ounces cream cheese, softened
1   tablespoon sugar
1/2   teaspoon instant coffee granules
1/2   teaspoon vanilla extract
1/4   cup miniature semisweet chocolate chips

MUFFINS

Mix the flour, sugar, baking powder, cinnamon and salt in a bowl. Dissolve the coffee granules in the milk in a bowl. Add the butter, egg and vanilla and mix well. Add to the dry ingredients and stir just until moistened. Fold in the chocolate chips. Fill greased or paper-lined muffin cups two-thirds full. Bake at 375 degrees for 17 to 20 minutes or until the muffins test done. Cool in the pan for 5 minutes. Remove to a wire rack to cool completely.

TOPPING

Combine the cream cheese, sugar, coffee granules and vanilla in a bowl and mix well. Stir in the chocolate chips. Spread over the tops of the cooled muffins.

MAKES 14

Amaretto Almond Bread

1/2	cup (1 stick) butter, softened
1/2	cup sugar
3	egg yolks
1	cup sifted all-purpose flour
1/4	cup amaretto
1	teaspoon black walnut flavoring
1/3	cup sliced almonds
3	egg whites
1/2	cup sugar

Beat the butter and 1/2 cup sugar in a bowl until light and fluffy. Add the egg yolks and beat well. Beat in the flour alternately with the liqueur. Stir in the black walnut flavoring and almonds. Beat the egg whites in a mixing bowl until soft peaks form. Add 1/2 cup sugar and beat until stiff peaks form. Fold the egg whites into the batter. Pour into a well-greased loaf pan. Bake at 350 degrees for 45 minutes or until the bread tests done. Cool in the pan for 10 minutes. Remove to a wire rack to cool completely.

MAKES 8 SERVINGS

Rogers Little Theater has been entertaining community theater patrons for more than twenty years. Events such as musicals, dramas, and youth talent shows are offered throughout the year. Rogers Little Theater is housed in the refurbished Victory Theater, which opened in 1927 as the first motion picture theater in Northwest Arkansas.

Honey Banana Bread

3/4	cup all-purpose flour
3/4	cup quick-cooking oats
1	teaspoon baking powder
1/2	teaspoon salt
1/2	teaspoon nutmeg
1/4	teaspoon cinnamon
1/2	cup honey
1/3	cup butter, softened
1	teaspoon vanilla extract
2	eggs
4	ripe bananas, mashed

Mix the flour, oats, baking powder, salt, nutmeg and cinnamon together. Beat the honey and butter in a mixing bowl until light and fluffy. Beat in the vanilla. Add the eggs, one at a time, beating well after each addition. Beat in the dry ingredients alternately with the bananas. Spoon into a greased and floured loaf pan. Bake at 325 degrees for 50 to 55 minutes or until a wooden pick inserted in the center comes out clean. Cool in the pan for 15 minutes. Remove to a wire rack to cool completely.

MAKES 10 TO 12 SERVINGS

Morning Glory Bread

2	cups sugar
4	cups all-purpose flour
4	teaspoons baking soda
4	teaspoons cinnamon
1	teaspoon salt
1	cup raisins
1	cup chopped apples
4	cups grated carrots
1	cup canned shredded coconut
1	cup chopped pecans
6	eggs, lightly beaten
1½	cups vegetable oil
1	teaspoon vanilla extract

Combine the sugar, flour, baking soda, cinnamon and salt in a large bowl and mix well. Add the raisins, apples, carrots, coconut and pecans, tossing after each addition to coat with the dry ingredients. Add the eggs, oil and vanilla and stir just until combined. Pour into three greased small loaf pans or fill greased muffin cups two-thirds full. Bake the loaves at 350 degrees for 1 hour or the muffins at 375 degrees for 20 to 30 minutes or until the muffins test done. Cool in the pans for 10 minutes. Remove to a wire rack to cool completely.

MAKES 3 SMALL LOAVES OR 2 DOZEN MUFFINS

Strawberry Bread

1½	cups all-purpose flour
1	cup sugar
½	teaspoon baking soda
½	teaspoon salt
½	teaspoon cinnamon
2	eggs
1	cup frozen strawberries, thawed and undrained
2/3	cup vegetable oil
½	cup chopped toasted walnuts

Combine the flour, sugar, baking soda, salt and cinnamon in a bowl. Make a well in the center and add the eggs, strawberries and oil and mix well. Stir in the walnuts and pour into a greased loaf pan. Bake at 350 degrees for 40 to 45 minutes or until the bread tests done. Cool in the pan for 10 minutes. Remove to a wire rack to cool.

MAKES 8 SERVINGS

Perfect Pan Corn Bread

1	cup all-purpose flour
1	cup yellow cornmeal
¼	cup sugar
1	tablespoon baking powder
½	teaspoon salt
¼	cup shortening
2	eggs, lightly beaten
1	cup milk

Mix the flour, cornmeal, sugar, baking powder and salt together. Melt the shortening in a 10½-inch cast-iron skillet in a 425-degree oven for 5 minutes; do not burn. Combine the eggs and milk in a bowl and mix well. Add the shortening and mix well. Add the dry ingredients and stir just until smooth. Pour into the hot skillet and bake at 425 degrees for 20 to 25 minutes or until the bottom is brown.

MAKES 6 SERVINGS

Feta Cumin Corn Bread

1½	cups yellow cornmeal
1	cup all-purpose flour
2	teaspoons baking powder
½	teaspoon baking soda
1	teaspoon salt
2	teaspoons cumin
1½	cups (6 ounces) crumbled feta cheese
1	cup thinly sliced green onions
2	eggs
1	cup milk
2	tablespoons sugar
¼	cup vegetable oil

Sift the cornmeal, flour, baking powder, baking soda, salt and cumin into a bowl. Add the cheese and green onions and mix well. Whisk the eggs, milk, sugar and oil in a bowl. Add to the feta mixture and stir just until combined. Pour into a greased loaf pan. Bake at 350 degrees for 45 to 50 minutes or until a wooden pick inserted in the center comes out clean. Cool in the pan for 5 minutes. Run a thin knife around the edge of the pan and remove the corn bread to a wire rack to cool completely.

MAKES 8 SERVINGS

Jalapeño Corn Muffins

1¹⁄₄   cups cornmeal
¹⁄₂   cup all-purpose flour
1   tablespoon sugar
2   teaspoons baking powder
1¹⁄₂   teaspoons salt
1   egg
³⁄₄   cup milk
¹⁄₄   cup vegetable oil
3 or   4 jalapeño chiles, chopped
1   onion, chopped
1   (15-ounce) can cream-style corn
1   cup (4 ounces) shredded sharp Cheddar cheese

Combine the cornmeal, flour, sugar, baking powder and salt in a bowl and mix well. Add the egg, milk, oil, jalapeño chiles, onion, corn and cheese and mix well. Fill lightly greased muffin cups two-thirds full. Bake at 425 degrees for 25 minutes. Remove to a wire rack to cool.

MAKES 12

Gen Broyles's Refrigerator Rolls

This dough can be refrigerated for up to seven days so you can bake rolls as needed.

1	cup boiling water
1/2	cup sugar
1	cup (2 sticks) margarine
2	eggs, beaten
1 1/2	teaspoons salt
2	envelopes dry yeast
1	cup warm water
6 to	7 cups all-purpose flour

Pour the boiling water over the sugar and margarine in a large heatproof bowl. Stir until the sugar is dissolved and the margarine is melted; let cool. Add the eggs and salt and mix well. Dissolve the yeast in the warm water in a bowl. Stir into the margarine mixture. Stir in the flour gradually to form a dough. Chill, covered, overnight. Roll out the dough on a floured work surface to 1/4-inch thickness. Cut with a round cutter and fold each circle in half to make "pocketbook" rolls. Arrange the rolls 1/4 inch apart in a well-greased baking pan. Let rise in a warm place until doubled in bulk. Bake at 350 degrees for 15 minutes or until golden brown.

MAKES ABOUT 5 DOZEN

Two Fayetteville institutions were united in the marriage of the University of Arkansas Athletic Director Frank Broyles and the former Gen Whitehead. Both lost long-term spouses in recent years. Razorback fans have grown up with Coach Broyles and his positive impact on not just Arkansas football, but all U of A sports. Gen was a labor and delivery room nurse at Washington Regional Medical Center for more than thirty years. Together they continue a tradition of generous community service.

COME ON IN

Appetizers and Beverages

Spicy Chicken Dip

2	cups (8 ounces) shredded Monterey Jack cheese		1	(8-ounce) can chopped water chestnuts
3/4	cup chopped onion		1 1/2	cups chopped cooked chicken
8	ounces cream cheese, softened		1/4	cup chopped cilantro
1	(10-ounce) package frozen chopped spinach, thawed and well drained			Avocado slices, sour cream and additional Monterey Jack cheese for garnish
1/3	cup salsa			
2	cups chopped seeded tomatoes			

Combine 2 cups Monterey Jack cheese, the onion, cream cheese, spinach, salsa, tomatoes, water chestnuts, chicken and cilantro in a bowl and mix well. Spoon into a baking dish and bake at 400 degrees for 20 minutes. Garnish with avocado slices, sour cream and additional Monterey Jack cheese.

MAKES 36 SERVINGS

One of the most recognized landmarks in Northwest Arkansas is Old Main, the oldest building on the University of Arkansas campus. With its clock tower recently restored, Old Main continues to stand as a beacon of higher education, just as it has for the past 130 years.

Cool Cucumber Dip

8	ounces cream cheese, softened
1	cup sour cream
1	envelope ranch salad dressing mix
1	teaspoon lemon juice
2	cucumbers, peeled, seeded and finely chopped
1	cup (4 ounces) finely shredded Cheddar cheese

Combine the cream cheese, sour cream, salad dressing mix and lemon juice in a bowl and mix well. Stir in the cucumbers. Fold in the Cheddar cheese. Chill, covered, until ready to serve.

MAKES 18 SERVINGS

Beef Bread Bowl Dip

1	(2-ounce) jar dried beef, chopped
8	ounces cream cheese, softened
1	cup sour cream
1	(4-ounce) can chopped green chiles
2	cups (8 ounces) shredded sharp Cheddar cheese
1	round loaf Hawaiian bread or sourdough bread

Combine the beef, cream cheese, sour cream, green chiles and Cheddar cheese in a bowl and mix well. Cut the top off the bread and reserve. Hollow out the bread to make a bowl, reserving the bread chunks. Spoon the beef mixture into the bread bowl and replace the top. Place on a baking sheet and bake at 325 degrees for 1 hour. Serve the reserved bread with the dip.

MAKES 18 SERVINGS

PHOTO ON PAGE 75

Blue Cheese Ball

16	ounces cream cheese, softened
2	ounces crumbled blue cheese
12	ounces sharp Cheddar cheese, shredded
1	onion, chopped
2	garlic cloves, minced
2	tablespoons Worcestershire sauce
6	drops hot red pepper sauce
1	tablespoon mayonnaise (optional)
1	cup chopped pecans

Combine the cream cheese, blue cheese, Cheddar cheese, onion, garlic, Worcestershire sauce and hot sauce in a bowl and mix well. Stir in the mayonnaise if needed for the desired consistency. Shape into a ball and coat in the pecans. Chill, covered, for up to 24 hours.

MAKES 12 SERVINGS

Game Day Cheese Dip

2	cups (8 ounces) finely shredded Cheddar cheese
1$^1/_2$	cups (6 ounces) finely shredded mozzarella cheese
$^1/_4$	cup (1 ounce) grated Parmesan cheese
2	cups mayonnaise
1	cup sour cream
2	tablespoons dried onion flakes
$^1/_4$	teaspoon garlic powder

Combine the Cheddar cheese, mozzarella cheese, Parmesan cheese, mayonnaise, sour cream, onion flakes and garlic powder in a bowl and mix well. Chill for 30 minutes. Serve with tortilla chips or corn chips.

MAKES 10 TO 15 SERVINGS

Smoked Gouda Dip

8	ounces cream cheese, softened
2/3	cup mayonnaise
1	cup (4 ounces) shredded smoked Gouda cheese
6	green onions, sliced
2	tablespoons grated Parmesan cheese
1/2	teaspoon pepper

Beat the cream cheese and mayonnaise in a bowl until smooth. Fold in the Gouda cheese, green onions, Parmesan cheese and pepper. Chill, covered, until ready to serve.

MAKES 10 TO 12 SERVINGS

Green with Envy Dip

1	(6-ounce) can black olives
1	cup (4 ounces) shredded Monterey Jack cheese
1	(4-ounce) can chopped green chiles
1/4	cup chopped cilantro
1/2	cup Italian salad dressing
1	plum tomato, chopped
4	green onions, chopped

Drain the olives, reserving half the liquid. Chop the olives. Combine the olives, reserved olive liquid, cheese, green chiles and cilantro in a bowl and mix well. Add the salad dressing, tomato and green onions and mix well. Chill for 1 hour. Serve with chips.

MAKES 12 SERVINGS

Zesty Spinach Dip

8	ounces frozen chopped spinach, thawed and well drained
8	ounces cream cheese, softened
2	cups (8 ounces) shredded sharp Cheddar cheese
1	(10-ounce) can tomatoes with green chiles

Combine the spinach, cream cheese, Cheddar cheese and tomatoes with green chiles in a bowl and mix well. Spoon into an 8×8-inch baking dish and bake at 350 degrees for 30 minutes. Serve warm with crackers or pita bread.

MAKES 16 SERVINGS

Sweet Dip for Fresh Fruit

8	ounces cream cheese, softened
9	ounces whipped topping
2	cups marshmallow creme
1/2	teaspoon vanilla extract

Combine the cream cheese and whipped topping in a bowl and mix well. Add the marshmallow creme and vanilla and mix well. Chill for at least 1 hour. Serve with fresh fruit.

MAKES 8 TO 10 SERVINGS

Serve dips from hollowed peppers, small cabbages, round bread loaves, small pumpkins, melons, tomatoes, oranges, and apples.

Fall Color Pumpkin Dip

16   *ounces cream cheese, softened*
3   *cups confectioners' sugar*
1   *(30-ounce) can pumpkin*
1   *tablespoon ginger*
1   *tablespoon cinnamon*

Beat the cream cheese and confectioners' sugar in a bowl until smooth. Fold in the pumpkin, ginger and cinnamon. Spoon into a small hollowed pumpkin and serve with gingersnap cookies.

MAKES 24 SERVINGS

Autumn Brie with Fruit and Nuts

1   *(4$^1/_2$- to 5-pound) round brie cheese*
1   *cup golden raisins*
1   *cup sliced almonds, lightly toasted*
1   *cup dried apricots, coarsely chopped*
1   *cup hazelnuts, coarsely chopped*
$^1/_2$ *cup dried currants*
$^1/_2$ *cup walnuts, coarsely chopped*
3   *walnut halves*

Wrap the cheese tightly in plastic wrap and freeze for 30 minutes. Remove the plastic wrap and cut the rind from the top of the cheese. Score ten equal wedges on the top of the cheese with a sharp knife. Spread half the raisins, half the almonds, half the apricots, half the hazelnuts, all of the currants, all of the chopped walnuts, remaining raisins, remaining almonds, remaining apricots and remaining hazelnuts consecutively over one wedge each, pressing lightly into the cheese. Place the walnut halves onto the center of the cheese. Chill, covered, for 30 minutes. Let stand at room temperature for 30 minutes before serving.

MAKES 48 SERVINGS

Marinated Cheese

1/2	cup olive oil	1/2	teaspoon pepper
1/2	cup white wine vinegar	3	garlic cloves, minced
3	tablespoons chopped parsley	1	(2-ounce) jar pimento,
3	tablespoons chopped		drained
	green onions	1	(8-ounce) block sharp Cheddar
1	teaspoon sugar		cheese, thinly sliced
3/4	teaspoon dried basil	1	(8-ounce) block mozzarella
1/2	teaspoon salt		cheese, thinly sliced

Combine the olive oil, wine vinegar, parsley, green onions, sugar, basil, salt, pepper, garlic and pimentos in a jar with a tight-fitting lid and shake well. Arrange the Cheddar cheese slices and mozzarella cheese slices in a shallow serving dish. Pour the marinade evenly over the cheese. Chill, covered, for at least 8 hours.

MAKES 20 SERVINGS

French Herb Cheese

This is a delicious and economical version of boursin cheese.

8	ounces cream cheese, softened	1/4	teaspoon dried basil
1/2	cup (1 stick) butter, softened	1/4	teaspoon dried marjoram
3/4	teaspoon minced garlic	1/4	teaspoon dried thyme
1/2	teaspoon dried oregano	1/4	teaspoon pepper

Beat the cream cheese and butter in a mixing bowl until smooth. Add the garlic, oregano, basil, marjoram, thyme and pepper and mix well. Chill, covered, until cold. Bring to room temperature before serving.

MAKES 16 SERVINGS

Dickson Street Hummus

1	(15-ounce) can garbanzo beans	1/4	cup toasted sesame seeds
		2	teaspoons cumin
3	garlic cloves		Salt to taste
	Juice of 1 lemon	2	tablespoons (about) olive oil

Process the garbanzo beans, garlic, lemon juice, sesame seeds, cumin and salt in a blender. Add the olive oil in a fine stream, processing constantly until creamy. Serve with pita bread, pita chips or fresh vegetables.

MAKES 4 SERVINGS

> The entertainment center of Fayetteville, Dickson Street is home to several restaurants, clubs, shops, galleries, and the Walton Arts Center. Located near the University of Arkansas, it is a popular spot for college students and locals. Live music is available each weekend. Dickson Street is also the location for Fayetteville's seasonal festivals and holiday parades.

Vegetarian Mushroom Pâté

3	tablespoons butter		1	teaspoon dried thyme
1/3	cup chopped onion		1	teaspoon dried oregano
1/3	cup chopped celery		1/2	teaspoon dried rosemary
1/4	cup thinly sliced green onions		1/2	teaspoon salt
1	teaspoon minced garlic		1/2	teaspoon freshly ground pepper
4	cups thinly sliced fresh mushrooms		4	ounces cream cheese, softened
3/4	cup chopped walnuts		1	egg, lightly beaten
1	teaspoon dried basil		1/4	cup fresh bread crumbs

Heat the butter in a large skillet over medium-high heat until the foam subsides. Add the onion, celery, green onions and garlic and sauté for 4 minutes or until the vegetables are tender and golden brown. Increase the heat to high and stir in the mushrooms. Add the walnuts, basil, thyme, oregano, rosemary, salt and pepper and cook until the liquid has evaporated, stirring occasionally. Add the cream cheese and cook until the cream cheese is melted, stirring constantly. Remove from the heat and let cool slightly. Purée the mushroom mixture in a food processor. Add the egg and bread crumbs and process until smooth. Pour into a greased 1-quart baking dish and wrap the entire dish in foil. Bake at 350 degrees for 35 minutes. Remove to a rack and let cool; do not unwrap. Chill, wrapped, overnight. Run a thin knife around the edge of the baking dish and invert the pâté onto a serving dish. Serve with crackers or toast points.

MAKES 10 TO 12 SERVINGS

Plant wheat grass in shallow containers
a few weeks before your party. Trim to the desired length.
Use under glass plates of food or insert flower
tubes for a garden centerpiece.

Smoked Salmon Finger Sandwiches

1/2   *cup smoked salmon, finely chopped*
4   *ounces cream cheese, softened*
2   *tablespoons minced red onion*
   Juice of 1 lemon
   Freshly ground pepper to taste
8   *slices thin sandwich bread, crusts removed*

Combine the salmon, cream cheese, onion, lemon juice and pepper in a bowl and mix well. Spread over half the bread slices and top with the remaining bread slices. Slice each sandwich into three or four "fingers."

MAKES 6 TO 8 SERVINGS

Crab-Stuffed Mushrooms

12 to 15 *large mushrooms*
4   *green onions, chopped*
1   *teaspoon minced garlic*
7   *tablespoons butter*
8   *ounces fresh or canned crab meat,*
   drained and flaked
1   *tablespoon chopped parsley*
1/2   *cup dry white wine*
1/2   *cup Italian-style seasoned bread crumbs*
1   *tablespoon butter, melted*
1/2   *cup (2 ounces) shredded fresh Parmesan cheese*

Remove the stems from the mushrooms and chop the stems. Sauté the green onions and garlic in 7 tablespoons butter in a skillet until tender. Stir in the mushroom stems, crab meat, parsley, wine and bread crumbs and cook over low heat for a few minutes, stirring constantly. Pour 1 tablespoon butter into a 9×13-inch baking pan and tilt the pan to coat the bottom. Arrange the mushroom caps top side down in the baking pan and spoon the stuffing into the mushroom caps. Sprinkle with the cheese and bake at 350 degrees for 15 minutes. Serve hot.

MAKES 6 SERVINGS

Crab English Muffins

8 ounces fresh or canned crab meat,
  drained and flaked
1/2 cup mayonnaise
1 tablespoon lemon juice
1 tablespoon minced onion
1/4 teaspoon Worcestershire sauce
  Dash of Tabasco sauce
  Dash of salt
  Dash of paprika
3 ounces cream cheese, softened
6 English muffins, split
1/3 to 1/2 cup grated Parmesan cheese

Combine the crab meat, mayonnaise, lemon juice, onion, Worcestershire sauce, Tabasco sauce, salt, paprika and cream cheese in a bowl and mix well. Spread equal portions of the crab mixture over the muffin halves. Spoon equal portions of the Parmesan cheese onto the center of each muffin half and arrange on a baking sheet. Cook under a broiler until golden brown, watching carefully.

MAKES 12 SERVINGS

Greek Shrimp

1 1/2 pounds deveined peeled large shrimp
6 tablespoons olive oil
3 tablespoons lemon juice
1/2 cup chopped fresh dill weed
2 large garlic cloves, minced
3 tablespoons capers
3 green onions, chopped
1 lemon, sliced for garnish
3 or 4 dill weed sprigs for garnish

Sauté the shrimp in 2 tablespoons of the olive oil in a skillet for 2 minutes or until the shrimp turn pink. Remove from the heat. Whisk the remaining 4 tablespoons olive oil, the lemon juice, chopped dill weed, garlic, capers and green onions in a bowl. Add the shrimp and toss to coat. Chill, covered, for 4 to 24 hours. Serve the shrimp on a serving platter and garnish with the lemon slices and dill weed sprigs.

MAKES 12 SERVINGS

Cinnamon Pecans

1	cup sugar
1/2	cup water
3/4	teaspoon salt
1	teaspoon vanilla extract
1	teaspoon cinnamon
3	cups pecan halves

Mix the sugar, water, salt and vanilla in a saucepan. Bring to a boil over medium heat and cook for 4 minutes. Remove from the heat and add the cinnamon and pecans. Stir until the syrup forms a sugary coating. Spread the pecans in a single layer over parchment paper and let cool.

MAKES 12 SERVINGS

Sweet-and-Spicy Pecans

2	egg whites
2	teaspoons salt
3/4	cup sugar
1	teaspoon cayenne pepper, or to taste
1 1/2	teaspoons Worcestershire sauce
4 1/2	cups pecan halves
6	tablespoons butter, melted and cooled

Beat the egg whites and salt in a bowl until foamy. Beat in the sugar, cayenne pepper and Worcestershire sauce. Fold in the pecans and butter. Spread the pecans evenly on a nonstick baking sheet. Bake at 325 degrees for 30 to 40 minutes or until crisp and toasted, stirring every 10 minutes. Remove to a wire rack to cool. Store in an airtight container.

MAKES 4 1/2 CUPS

Mocha Punch

12   *cups hot strong brewed coffee*
1¼ *cups sugar*
1   *cup chocolate syrup*
1   *tablespoon vanilla extract*
1   *teaspoon almond extract*
1   *gallon milk*
1   *quart vanilla ice cream*

Combine the coffee, sugar and chocolate syrup in a 2-gallon heatproof pitcher. Stir until the sugar is dissolved. Chill, covered, overnight. Stir in the vanilla, almond extract and milk. Scoop the ice cream into a punch bowl and pour the coffee mixture over the ice cream. You may use 2 percent milk, but whole milk provides a better flavor.

MAKES 25 TO 30 SERVINGS

Cranberry Tea

12   *ounces fresh or frozen cranberries*
8   *cups water*
2   *cups sugar*
3   *cinnamon sticks*
2   *cups water*
1   *(6-ounce) can frozen orange juice concentrate*
3   *ounces frozen lemonade concentrate*
2¼ *cups water*

Combine the cranberries and 8 cups water in a saucepan. Cook over medium-low heat for 10 to 20 minutes or until the cranberries are very soft. Push the cranberry mixture through a wire mesh strainer into a large bowl and discard the skins. Combine the sugar, cinnamon sticks and 2 cups water in a saucepan. Cook over medium-high heat for 8 to 10 minutes or until the sugar is dissolved, stirring frequently. Add to the cranberries. Add the orange juice concentrate, lemonade concentrate and 2¼ cups water and stir until the concentrates are melted. Let cool and then remove the cinnamon sticks. Pour into a pitcher and store in the refrigerator. Reheat when ready to serve.

MAKES 10 TO 12 SERVINGS

Cranberry Margaritas

1   *(12-ounce) can frozen limeade*
concentrate, thawed
1   *(12-ounce) can frozen cranberry juice*
cocktail concentrate, thawed
12   *ounces (1½ cups) tequila*
24   *ounces water*
4 to *8 ounces (½ to 1 cup) lemon-lime soda or club soda*
       Coarse salt
       Lime wedges for garnish

Pour the limeade concentrate, cranberry juice cocktail concentrate, tequila and water into a double-bagged 1-gallon sealable plastic freezer bag. (Use the empty juice cans to measure the water.) Seal the bags and place flat in the freezer for at least 24 to 48 hours. When ready to serve, pour the tequila mixture into a pitcher and stir in the soda. Serve in salt-rimmed glasses and garnish with lime wedges if desired.

MAKES 6 TO 8 SERVINGS

Riesling Sangria

1   *(750-milliliter) bottle riesling*
1½   *cups white cranberry-peach juice*
½   *cup peach schnapps*
3   *tablespoons fresh lemon juice*
2   *tablespoons sugar*
1   *teaspoon vanilla extract*
2   *(½-inch-thick) lemon slices*
2   *(½-inch-thick) orange slices*
2   *fresh peaches, cut into wedges, or*
frozen peach wedges
10   *fresh raspberries*
3   *cups ice cubes*

Mix the wine, white cranberry-peach juice, schnapps, lemon juice, sugar and vanilla in a large pitcher. Stir in the lemon slices, orange slices, peaches and raspberries. Chill, covered, overnight. Stir in the ice and serve.

MAKES 8 SERVINGS

Wedding Punch

3	cups boiling water		1	cup lemon juice
3	cups sugar		3	cups pineapple juice
3	cups boiling water		6	cups ginger ale
1/4	cup loose tea leaves			Maraschino cherries and
3	cups orange juice			mint sprigs for garnish

Combine 3 cups boiling water and the sugar in a saucepan and stir until the sugar is dissolved. Bring to a boil and boil for 7 minutes without stirring. Remove from the heat and let cool. Pour into a large pitcher. Pour 3 cups boiling water over the tea in a heatproof bowl. Let stand, covered, for 5 minutes. Strain through a wire mesh strainer into a heatproof bowl and let cool. Add the tea to the sugar syrup in the pitcher. Add the orange juice, lemon juice and pineapple juice and mix well. Chill until cold. Pour over ice in a punch bowl and stir in the ginger ale. Garnish with maraschino cherries and mint sprigs.

MAKES 50 SERVINGS

Frosty Mug Root Beer

1	gallon water
2	cups sugar
2	tablespoons root beer extract

Combine the water, sugar and root beer extract in a large jar. Stir until the sugar is dissolved. Chill, covered, until cold. Serve in frosted mugs on a hot day.

MAKES 16 SERVINGS

When creating an ice mold for a punch bowl, use a carbonated beverage, fruit juice tea, or tea in the mold in lieu of water. They will add flavor as they melt and will not dilute the punch. Add whole strawberries, cranberries, mint leaves, or citrus slices to the mold for additional impact.

Five-Generation Eggnog

6	egg whites
1/2	cup sugar
6	egg yolks
1/4	cup sugar
2	cups half-and-half
1	cup heavy cream
1	cup bourbon (optional)
1/2	cup rum (optional)
	Nutmeg

Beat the egg whites and 1/2 cup sugar in a large bowl until stiff peaks form. Beat the egg yolks and 1/4 cup sugar in a small bowl. Add the egg yolks to the egg whites, beating constantly.

Add the half-and-half and cream to the egg mixture, beating constantly. Beat in the bourbon and rum gradually until of the desired consistency. Pour into glasses and sprinkle each with a dash of nutmeg.

MAKES 8 SERVINGS

Note: If you are concerned about using raw eggs, use eggs pasteurized in their shells, which are sold at some specialty food stores, or use an equivalent amount of pasteurized egg yolk and pasteurized egg white.

Whiskey Sour Punch

1	(750-milliliter) bottle bourbon
2	(12-ounce) cans frozen orange juice concentrate, thawed
1	(6-ounce) can frozen lemonade concentrate, thawed
1	(46-ounce) can pineapple juice
1	(2-liter) bottle ginger ale

Combine the bourbon, orange juice concentrate, lemonade concentrate, pineapple juice and ginger ale in a large sealable freezer container and mix well. Seal the container and freeze until slushy. Spoon into glasses and serve.

MAKES 20 SERVINGS

FOR STARTERS

~ ❧ ~

Soups and Salads

Black Bean Soup

2	(15-ounce) cans black beans, drained and rinsed	1	(10-ounce) can condensed chicken broth
1	(15-ounce) can chopped tomatoes	2	(4-ounce) cans green chiles
1	(15-ounce) can tomatoes with green chiles	1½	cups frozen corn kernels
		4	green onions, sliced
		2	tablespoons chili powder
		2	teaspoons cumin

Combine the beans, chopped tomatoes, tomatoes with green chiles, broth, green chiles, corn, green onions, chili powder and cumin in a slow cooker and mix well. Cook, covered, on Low for 7 to 9 hours.

MAKES 8 SERVINGS

Fiesta Soup

4	boneless chicken breasts, chopped	1	(15-ounce) can whole kernel corn, drained
3	tablespoons olive oil	1	(15-ounce) can black beans
1	white or yellow onion, chopped	1	(15-ounce) can pinto beans
1	garlic clove, minced	4	cups chicken broth
1	tablespoon chili powder	1	tablespoon lime juice
1	teaspoon salt	½	cup crushed corn chips
1	teaspoon cumin	½	cup (2 ounces) shredded Cheddar cheese
1/8	teaspoon cayenne pepper	8 to	10 tablespoons guacamole
1	(4-ounce) can green chiles	8 to	10 tablespoons sour cream
1	(15-ounce) can diced tomatoes		

Sauté the chicken in the olive oil in a stockpot until the chicken is cooked through. Add the onion, garlic, chili powder, salt, cumin and cayenne pepper and sauté until the onion is tender. Stir in the green chiles, tomatoes, corn, black beans, pinto beans and broth. Simmer for 30 minutes or until heated through or cook for up to 8 hours in a slow cooker. Stir in the lime juice just before serving. Ladle into serving bowls and top with equal portions of the chips, cheese, guacamole and sour cream.

MAKES 8 TO 10 SERVINGS

English Cheddar Chowder

2	cups water
2	teaspoons salt
1/3	cup finely chopped carrots
1/3	cup finely chopped celery
1/3	cup minced onion
1	onion, minced
1/2	cup (1 stick) butter
3/4	cup all-purpose flour
4	cups milk
4	cups chicken stock
16	ounces sharp Cheddar cheese, shredded
1	teaspoon mustard
	Salt, black pepper and cayenne pepper to taste

Bring the water and salt to a boil in a saucepan. Add the carrots, celery and 1/3 cup onion and boil for 5 minutes. Remove from the heat. Sauté 1 onion in the butter in a stockpot until tender. Stir in the flour and cook for a few minutes, stirring constantly. Whisk in the milk and stock gradually. Whisk in the cheese and cooked vegetables with liquid. Season with mustard, salt, black pepper and cayenne pepper. Cook until the cheese is melted, whisking constantly. Bring to a simmer and serve.

MAKES 10 TO 12 SERVINGS

Corn Chowder

2	cups chopped potatoes
1	(14-ounce) can cream-style corn
1	(15-ounce) can whole kernel corn
1	cup half-and-half
1	cup cubed Velveeta cheese
8 to	10 slices bacon, crisp-cooked and crumbled
	Salt and pepper to taste

Cook the potatoes in a saucepan of boiling water for 15 to 20 minutes or until tender; drain well. Combine the potatoes, cream-style corn, whole kernel corn and half-and-half in a saucepan. Simmer, covered, for 20 to 30 minutes, stirring occasionally. Stir in the cheese. Stir in the bacon, salt and pepper. Cook until heated through, stirring occasionally.

MAKES 6 SERVINGS

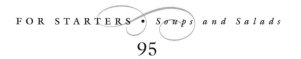

Crab Bisque

1   *(10-ounce) can condensed cream of*
      asparagus or cream of celery soup
1   *(10-ounce) can condensed cream of*
      mushroom soup
2²/3   *cups (about) milk*
1   *cup light cream*
      Cayenne pepper to taste
¹/2   *small onion, grated*
2   *tablespoons butter*
1   *cup fresh or canned crab meat,*
      drained and flaked
3/4   *cup sherry*
3   *tablespoons chopped parsley*

Combine the asparagus soup, mushroom soup, milk, cream and cayenne pepper in a saucepan and mix well. Sauté the onion in the butter in a skillet until tender. Stir in the crab meat. Add to the soup mixture and mix well. Bring just to a boil, stirring frequently. Stir in the sherry and simmer for a few minutes. Ladle into serving bowls and top with equal portions of the parsley.

MAKES 6 TO 8 SERVINGS

Vegetarian French Onion Soup

16   *ounces white onions, thinly sliced*
2   *cups dry white wine*
2   *tablespoons unsalted butter*
6   *cups vegetable broth*
6   *(¹/2-inch-thick) slices crusty baguette, toasted*
2   *cups (8 ounces) shredded Gruyère cheese*

Combine the onions, wine and butter in a 9×13-inch baking dish and mix well. Bake at 425 degrees for 45 to 60 minutes or until the onion is very soft and most of the liquid is absorbed. Bring the broth to a simmer in a saucepan. Divide the onion mixture among six heatproof serving bowls and top each with 1 cup of the hot broth. Place one bread slice over each bowl of soup and top with equal portions of the cheese. Broil for 2 to 3 minutes or until the cheese is melted.

MAKES 6 SERVINGS

Seafood Gumbo

1	cup all-purpose flour	1	(14-ounce) can
1	cup vegetable oil		chopped tomatoes
3	white or yellow	1	(16-ounce) bag frozen okra
	onions, chopped	2	(12-ounce) cans chunk chicken
5	ribs celery, chopped	2 or	3 (6-ounce) cans crab meat,
2	tablespoons vegetable oil		drained and flaked
8	cups chicken broth	2	pounds deveined peeled
1	(24-ounce) jar hot		medium shrimp
	picante sauce		Hot cooked rice

Mix the flour and 1 cup oil in a cast-iron skillet. Bake at 350 degrees for 1 to 1½ hours or until medium brown or cook in a saucepan until medium brown, stirring constantly. Sauté the onions and celery in 2 tablespoons oil in a stockpot until tender. Stir in the flour mixture, broth, picante sauce, tomatoes, okra, chicken and crab meat. Simmer for 1 hour, stirring occasionally. Stir in the shrimp and simmer for 20 to 30 minutes. Serve over rice.

MAKES 10 TO 12 SERVINGS

Creamy Potato Soup

3 or	4 russet potatoes, peeled		Celery salt to taste
	and chopped		Pepper to taste
2	ribs celery, finely chopped	½	cup half-and-half
2	carrots, finely shredded		Dash of cinnamon
½	small yellow onion, minced	1	cup (4 ounces) shredded
1	teaspoon salt		Cheddar cheese
4 to	5 cups water	½	cup crumbled
2	tablespoons butter		crisp-cooked bacon

Combine the potatoes, celery, carrots, onion and salt in a stockpot. Add enough of the water to cover. Cook until the vegetables are tender. Mash the vegetables in the stockpot. Stir in the butter, celery salt, pepper, half-and-half and cinnamon. Cook until heated through. Ladle into serving bowls and top with equal portions of the cheese and bacon.

MAKES 4 TO 6 SERVINGS

Curried Pumpkin Peanut Soup

2	tablespoons vegetable oil
1	yellow onion, chopped
1	apple, peeled and chopped
3	tablespoons curry powder
1/2	cup creamy peanut butter
2	cups canned pumpkin
2	cups chicken broth
1	teaspoon salt
1/4	teaspoon cayenne pepper, or to taste
1	cup chicken broth
1	cup half-and-half
1/2	cup chopped peanuts

Heat the oil in a stockpot and stir in the onion. Cook, covered, until the onion is tender. Stir in the apple and cook, covered, until the apple is tender. Stir in the curry powder and peanut butter. Add the pumpkin and mix well. Stir in 2 cups broth, the salt and cayenne pepper. Simmer, covered, for 15 minutes. Stir in 1 cup broth and the half-and-half. Cook until heated through; do not let boil. Adjust seasonings to taste. Ladle into serving bowls and top with equal portions of the peanuts.

MAKES 6 SERVINGS

The Arts Center of the Ozarks (ACO) was the first community arts organization in Northwest Arkansas. Located in Springdale, ACO recently celebrated its fortieth anniversary. An annual highlight of the ACO calendar is the summer musical, in which the Broadway talent of local performers is showcased to sell-out crowds. Recent productions include Guys and Dolls, Camelot, and Big River. Other dramatic productions are held throughout the year. ACO provides entertainment and educational opportunities for the entire family.

Taco Salad

1	pound ground beef
1	onion, minced
1	envelope taco seasoning mix
1	head iceberg lettuce, shredded
1	large tomato, chopped
16	ounces Cheddar cheese, shredded
1	(6-ounce) can chopped black olives, drained
1	(15-ounce) can ranch-style beans, drained and rinsed
1	large package corn chips
1	(16-ounce) bottle French Catalina salad dressing, or to taste

Brown the ground beef with the onion in a skillet, stirring until the ground beef is crumbly; drain. Add the seasoning mix and cook according to the package directions. Combine the lettuce, tomato, cheese, olives and beans in a large bowl and toss to mix. Top with the meat mixture and corn chips. Pour the salad dressing over the top and serve.

MAKES 6 SERVINGS

Debbie Walker's Taco Salad

1 1/2	pounds lean ground beef
1	envelope taco seasoning mix
1	(13-ounce) bag nacho cheese tortilla chips, crushed
1	bell pepper, chopped
2	tomatoes, chopped
1	(15-ounce) can kidney beans, drained and rinsed
1	(6-ounce) can sliced black olives, drained
3	cups (12 ounces) shredded 2% milk cheese
1	(16-ounce) bottle light ranch salad dressing
	Poppy seeds to taste
1	(8-ounce) bag salad greens

Brown the ground beef in a skillet, stirring until crumbly; drain. Add the seasoning mix and cook according to the package directions. Layer the tortilla chips, meat mixture, bell pepper, tomatoes, beans, olives, cheese, salad dressing and poppy seeds in the order listed one-third at a time in a large baking dish. Bake at 350 degrees for 30 minutes or until heated through. Serve warm over the salad greens.

MAKES 8 TO 10 SERVINGS

Chicken Poppy Seed Pasta Salad

16	ounces penne, cooked al dente and drained	1	red onion, chopped
1¼	pounds chicken breast strips, cooked, or 3 or 4 chicken breasts, cooked and cut into strips	¾	cup mayonnaise
		1	cup bottled poppy seed salad dressing
		1	teaspoon salt
¾	cup chopped celery	½	teaspoon pepper
1	(6-ounce) package sweetened dried cranberries	4	cups fresh baby spinach, chopped
		1	cup toasted walnuts

Combine the pasta, chicken, celery, cranberries and onion in a large bowl and toss to mix. Combine the mayonnaise, salad dressing, salt and pepper in a bowl and mix well. Fold into the chicken mixture. Chill, covered, for several hours to overnight. Serve the chicken salad over the spinach and sprinkle with the walnuts.

MAKES 16 SERVINGS

Thai Chicken Salad

3	pounds boneless chicken breasts	1	bunch cilantro, chopped
			Juice of 5 lemons
4	cups chicken broth	½	(13-ounce) can coconut milk
3	tablespoons flaked coconut	6	ribs celery, sliced diagonally
1	tablespoon red pepper flakes	5	green onions, sliced diagonally
1	(1-inch) piece fresh ginger, minced		Salt and pepper to taste
2	tablespoons sweet Thai chili sauce		Salad greens

Poach the chicken in the chicken broth in a saucepan until cooked through. Drain and let cool. Slice or shred the chicken. Combine the coconut and red pepper flakes in a saucepan. Cook until the coconut is lightly toasted, stirring constantly. Combine the chicken, coconut mixture, ginger, chili sauce, most of the cilantro (reserving some for garnish), lemon juice and coconut milk in a bowl and toss to mix. Add the celery, green onions, salt and pepper and toss to mix. Serve over salad greens and garnish with the reserved cilantro.

MAKES 6 TO 8 SERVINGS

Swatow Chicken Salad

1/3	cup soy sauce	1	can baby corn, drained and cut into 1-inch pieces
2	tablespoons cornstarch		
2	tablespoons sesame oil	1	can bamboo shoots, drained
3	boneless skinless chicken breasts, cut into bite-size pieces	1	tablespoon vegetable oil
		1	tablespoon mayonnaise
3	boneless skinless chicken thighs, cut into bite-size pieces	1	tablespoon vegetable oil
		1	(10-ounce) bag salad greens
6	green onions, sliced	1	(5-ounce) can chow mein noodles
1	red bell pepper, julienned		
1	can straw mushrooms, drained	1	bunch cilantro, or 1 (11-ounce) can mandarin oranges, drained, for garnish
1	can water chestnuts, drained and sliced		

Mix the soy sauce, cornstarch and sesame oil in a bowl. Add the chicken and stir to coat. Chill for 1 to 2 hours. Stir-fry the green onions, bell pepper, mushrooms, water chestnuts, corn and bamboo shoots in 1 tablespoon vegetable oil in a nonstick skillet until the green onions and bell pepper are tender-crisp. Remove to a large bowl and stir in the mayonnaise. Heat 1 tablespoon vegetable oil in the skillet. Add the chicken with marinade and sauté until the chicken is cooked through. Stir into the vegetable mixture. Spread the salad greens over a serving platter and top with the chow mein noodles. Spread the chicken salad over the noodles and garnish with the cilantro or mandarin oranges.

MAKES 8 SERVINGS

Sweet and Savory Broccoli Salad

1	cup mayonnaise	2	bunches broccoli florets, cut into bite-size pieces
1/2	cup (2 ounces) grated Parmesan cheese		
		1/2	cup golden raisins
1/3	cup sugar	10	slices bacon, crisp-cooked and crumbled
1	tablespoon red wine vinegar		
1/2	red onion, minced	1/2	cup toasted sunflower seeds

Mix the mayonnaise, cheese, sugar and wine vinegar in a bowl. Combine the onion, broccoli, raisins, bacon and sunflower seeds in a bowl and toss to mix. Add the mayonnaise mixture and toss to coat. Chill, covered, for at least 2 hours.

MAKES 8 SERVINGS

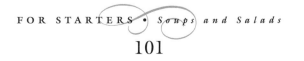

Tailgate Corn Bread Salad

1	package corn bread mix
1	(14-ounce) can whole kernel corn, drained
1/2	cup picante sauce
2	cups sour cream
1/2	cup mayonnaise
1	small purple onion, chopped
1	small green bell pepper, chopped
1	(3-ounce) can chopped black olives
2	cups (8 ounces) shredded sharp Cheddar cheese

Prepare the corn bread mix and bake according to the package directions. Cool and break into pieces in a large bowl. Combine the corn, picante sauce, sour cream, mayonnaise, onion, bell pepper, olives and cheese in a bowl and mix well. Fold into the corn bread. Chill, covered, until cold.

MAKES 12 SERVINGS

Ozark Potato Salad

3	pounds potatoes, cooked and chopped
3	ribs celery, chopped
1	small red onion, chopped
1/3	cup chopped dill pickles
1	cup mayonnaise
1	tablespoon yellow mustard
1	tablespoon Dijon mustard
1 1/2	teaspoons dill pickle juice
1/2	teaspoon celery salt
	Salt and pepper to taste

Combine the potatoes, celery, onion and dill pickles in a bowl and mix well. Combine the mayonnaise, yellow mustard, Dijon mustard, pickle juice, celery salt, salt and pepper in a bowl and mix well. Add to the potato mixture and mix well.

MAKES 8 SERVINGS

Marinated Vegetable Salad

1	(14-ounce) can tiny peas, drained	1/2 to 1	cup chopped onion
1	(14-ounce) can white Shoe Peg corn, drained	1	(2-ounce) jar diced pimento
1	(15-ounce) can cut green beans, drained	1/2	cup white vinegar
		1/2	cup vegetable oil
1	cup chopped celery	3/4	cup sugar
1	cup chopped green bell pepper	1	teaspoon salt
		1	teaspoon pepper

Combine the peas, corn, beans, celery, bell pepper, onion and pimentos in a bowl and mix gently. Mix the vinegar, oil, sugar, salt and pepper in a microwave-safe bowl. Microwave on High for 3 to 4 minutes and stir well. Pour over the vegetables. Chill, covered, overnight, stirring gently once or twice. Drain and serve.

MAKES 8 SERVINGS

Caesar Salad

3	garlic cloves, crushed	1	large head romaine, torn into bite-size pieces
1/4	cup olive oil		
1	teaspoon Worcestershire sauce	1/2	lemon
1/2	teaspoon salt	1/4	cup (1 ounce) freshly grated Parmesan cheese
1/4	teaspoon dry mustard		
1	teaspoon anchovy paste		Freshly ground pepper to taste

Rub the garlic on the inside of a wooden salad bowl and leave the garlic in the bowl. Add the olive oil, Worcestershire sauce, salt, dry mustard and anchovy paste and mix well. Add the romaine and toss until the leaves glisten. Squeeze the lemon over the romaine and toss to coat. Add the cheese and toss to mix. Season with pepper and serve immediately.

MAKES 6 SERVINGS

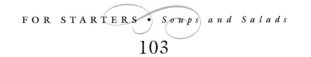

Bacon and Mandarin Salad

1/2	cup olive oil	1	bunch red leaf lettuce,	
1/4	cup red wine vinegar		torn into bite-size pieces	
1/4	cup sugar	1	head romaine, torn into	
1	tablespoon chopped fresh basil		bite-size pieces	
1/8	teaspoon hot red pepper sauce	1	pound bacon, crisp-cooked	
2	(15-ounce) cans mandarin		and crumbled	
	oranges, drained and chilled	4	ounces sliced toasted almonds	

Whisk the olive oil, wine vinegar, sugar, basil and hot sauce in a large bowl. Add the oranges, red leaf lettuce and romaine and toss gently to coat. Sprinkle with the bacon and almonds and serve immediately.

MAKES 8 SERVINGS

Strawberry Spinach Salad

This dressing can be doubled and stored in the refrigerator for up to four weeks.

SPINACH SALAD DRESSING

1/2	cup sugar or Splenda
2	tablespoons sesame seeds, toasted
1	tablespoon poppy seeds
1/4	teaspoon paprika
1/2	teaspoon dried onion flakes
1/2	cup olive oil
1/4	cup cider vinegar

SALAD

2	bunches fresh spinach, or 1 large bag fresh spinach
1 to 2	pints strawberries, sliced

DRESSING

Combine the sugar, sesame seeds, poppy seeds, paprika, onion flakes, olive oil and cider vinegar in a jar with a tight-fitting lid and shake well.

SALAD

Combine the spinach and strawberries in a bowl. Add the dressing and toss to coat. Serve immediately.

MAKES 8 SERVINGS

PHOTO ON PAGE 93

Spinach and Sprout Salad with Bacon

CATALINA DRESSING

1	cup olive oil
1/2	cup red wine vinegar
1	onion, chopped
3/4	cup sugar
1	teaspoon Worcestershire sauce
1/3	cup ketchup
1	teaspoon salt

SALAD

20	ounces fresh spinach
1	can bean sprouts, drained
1	(8-ounce) can water chestnuts, chopped
4	hard-cooked eggs, chopped
1	pound bacon, crisp-cooked and crumbled

DRESSING

Process the olive oil, wine vinegar, onion, sugar, Worcestershire sauce, ketchup and salt in a blender.

SALAD

Combine the spinach, bean sprouts, water chestnuts, eggs and bacon in a bowl and toss to mix. Add the dressing and toss to coat.

MAKES 6 TO 8 SERVINGS

Southwest Couscous Salad

2	cups chicken broth or chicken stock	3	green onions, chopped	
2	cups frozen corn kernels	1/2	teaspoon salt	
1 1/2	cups couscous	1/4	teaspoon pepper	
3 to	4 boneless skinless chicken breasts, cooked and cut into bite-size pieces	1/4	cup chopped cilantro	
		1/4	cup lime juice	
		2	tablespoons olive oil	
1	cup chopped plum tomato	1	teaspoon cumin	
1/2	cup chopped green bell pepper	1	teaspoon hot red pepper sauce	
			Lime wedges for garnish	

Heat the broth to boiling in a saucepan. Add the corn and cook for 3 minutes. Stir in the couscous and remove from the heat. Let stand, covered, for 5 minutes. Fluff the mixture with a fork. Combine the couscous mixture, chicken, tomato, bell pepper and green onions in a bowl. Whisk the salt, pepper, cilantro, lime juice, olive oil, cumin and hot sauce in a bowl. Add to the chicken mixture and mix well. Garnish with lime wedges and serve immediately.

MAKES 6 SERVINGS

Fruited Chicken Pasta Salad

1¹/₃ cups pasta shells, cooked al dente, drained and cooled
2   cups bite-size pieces cooked chicken breasts
1   cup sliced celery
¹/₄   red onion, chopped
1   (8-ounce) can diced water chestnuts, drained
1   (11-ounce) can mandarin oranges, drained
1   cup seedless grapes, cut into halves
¹/₄   cup mayonnaise
¹/₄   cup ranch salad dressing
¹/₄   teaspoon salt
¹/₈   teaspoon pepper
¹/₈   teaspoon celery seeds

Combine the pasta, chicken, celery, onion, water chestnuts, oranges and grapes in a bowl and toss to mix. Combine the mayonnaise, salad dressing, salt, pepper and celery seeds in a bowl and mix well. Add to the pasta mixture and toss to coat.

MAKES 6 SERVINGS

Feta Pasta Salad

16   ounces medium pasta shells, cooked al dente and drained
2   (6-ounce) cans pitted medium black olives, drained
3   (7-ounce) jars pimento-stuffed green olives, drained
1   large red onion, minced
1   (16-ounce) bottle Italian salad dressing
1   cup olive oil
5   large tomatoes, chopped
1   (13-ounce) can artichoke heats, drained and sliced
8   ounces feta cheese, crumbled

Combine the pasta, black olives, green olives, onion, salad dressing and olive oil in a large bowl and mix gently. Chill, covered, for 6 hours to overnight. Add the tomatoes, artichokes and cheese and mix gently. Serve at room temperature or chill for 2 to 3 hours before serving.

MAKES 10 SERVINGS

Helen R. Walton's 24-Hour Salad

From the recipe files of Helen R. Walton:
"This is a salad recipe from my mother, Hazel Carr Robson, who lived and cooked delicious food for her family in Claremore, Oklahoma."

2	cups white cherries, pitted and cut into halves
2	cups chopped pineapple
2	cups orange sections
2	cups miniature marshmallows
4	ounces chopped blanched almonds
2	eggs
1/3	cup sugar
1/4	cup half-and-half
	Juice of 1 lemon
1	cup heavy whipping cream, whipped

Place the cherries, pineapple and orange sections in a colander and drain well. Remove to a bowl and add the marshmallows and almonds. Beat the eggs in a mixing bowl until light. Beat in the sugar, half-and-half and lemon juice gradually. Pour into the top of a double boiler and place over simmering water. Cook until thickened, stirring constantly. Remove from the heat and let the mixture cool. Fold in the whipped cream. Pour over the fruit mixture and mix gently. Chill, covered, for 24 hours.

MAKES 10 TO 12 SERVINGS

STAY FOR DINNER

Main Dishes

Foolproof Baked Brisket 110

Cantonese Ginger Beef 110

Slow-Cooked Pepper Beef 111

Picadillo 111

Barbecued Chicken 112

Chicken and Dumplings 112

Citrus Chicken 113

Tandoori Chicken 113

Honey Curry Chicken 114

Fried Chicken Tenders 114

Tyson Family Southern
Fried Chicken 115

Plum Chicken with Couscous 116
(pictured at right)

Helen R. Walton's
Christmas Quail 117

Halibut Parmesan 118

Grilled Feta Shrimp 118

Cream Cheese Shrimp 119

Shrimp Scampi 120

Wonderful Peppered Shrimp 120

Pat Walker's Chicken Spaghetti 121

Robin George's
Chicken Spaghetti 122

Company's Coming
White Lasagna 123

Rigatoni 124

Pistachio Pesto Pasta 124

Artichoke Chicken Pasta 125

Sun-Dried Tomato Pesto 125

Hot Sausage Pasta 126

Meaty Spaghetti Sauce 126

Fettuccine Alfredo 127

Weekend Navy Beans and
Ham 128

Football Season Muffulettas 129

Foolproof Baked Brisket

1   (5-pound) beef brisket, trimmed
1   teaspoon garlic salt
1   teaspoon onion salt
1   teaspoon celery salt
1   (4-ounce) bottle liquid smoke
2   cups ketchup
1/2   cup vinegar
1/2   cup sugar
1/2   cup Worcestershire sauce

Place the brisket in a large Dutch oven and sprinkle with the garlic salt, onion salt and celery salt. Reserve 4 teaspoons of the liquid smoke. Pour the remaining liquid smoke over the brisket. Chill, covered, overnight. Remove any excess liquid from the Dutch oven. Mix the reserved 4 teaspoons liquid smoke, the ketchup, vinegar, sugar and Worcestershire sauce in a saucepan and bring to a boil. Reduce the heat and simmer until the sugar dissolves, stirring frequently. Pour evenly over the brisket. Bake, covered, at 250 degrees for 5 to 6 hours or until the meat is easily pulled into shreds. Make another batch of sauce to serve with the brisket, if desired.

MAKES 6 TO 8 SERVINGS

Cantonese Ginger Beef

1/3   cup soy sauce
2 1/2   tablespoons cornstarch
3   tablespoons sesame oil
2   pounds top round steak, cut into bite-size pieces
3   tablespoons vegetable oil
8   ounces fresh ginger, peeled and julienned
1   bunch green onions, cut into 1 1/2-inch pieces

Whisk the soy sauce, cornstarch and sesame oil in a bowl. Add the beef and stir to coat. Chill for 1 to 2 hours, stirring occasionally. Heat the vegetable oil in a nonstick skillet. Add the ginger and stir-fry until light brown. Add the beef with marinade to the skillet. Cook, covered, until the beef is brown on the bottom. Turn the beef and cook, covered, until brown on the other side. Add the green onions and cook until the green onions are tender. Serve with hot steamed rice.

MAKES 8 SERVINGS

Slow-Cooked Pepper Beef

2 to	2½ pounds round steak, cut into 1×3-inch strips		½	teaspoon pepper
2	tablespoons vegetable oil		½	teaspoon ginger
½	cup soy sauce		1	(16-ounce) can diced tomatoes
1	onion, sliced		2	large green bell peppers, cut into strips
2	teaspoons minced garlic			Hot cooked rice or egg noodles
2	teaspoons sugar			
1	teaspoon salt			

Brown the beef in the oil in a skillet. Remove to a slow cooker. Mix the soy sauce, onion, garlic, sugar, salt, pepper and ginger in a bowl and pour over the beef. Cook, covered, on Low for 5 to 6 hours or until the beef is tender. Stir in the tomatoes and bell peppers. Cook, covered, on Low for 1 hour longer. Serve over hot rice or noodles.

MAKES 12 TO 14 SERVINGS

Picadillo

1½	pounds ground beef		1	tablespoon chopped parsley
1¾	cups chopped onions		2	tablespoons capers
¾	cup chopped green bell pepper		½	cup sliced green olives
1	tablespoon chopped garlic		½	cup white wine
2	tablespoons olive oil			Hot cooked white or yellow rice
1	(8-ounce) can tomato sauce			
	Salt and pepper to taste			

Brown the ground beef in a skillet, stirring until crumbly; drain. Sauté the onions, bell pepper and garlic in the olive oil in a skillet over medium heat until tender. Stir in the tomato sauce and cook for 10 minutes. Stir in the salt, pepper, parsley and ground beef. Cook for 20 minutes, stirring occasionally. Add the capers, olives and wine and cook for 15 minutes, stirring occasionally. Serve over white or yellow rice.

MAKES 6 SERVINGS

Barbecued Chicken

3	chickens, split	2	tablespoons cayenne pepper
	Salt and pepper to taste	2	tablespoons black pepper
3	cups cider vinegar	1	tablespoon garlic powder
1/4	cup (1/2 stick) butter	1	cup Worcestershire sauce
3	tablespoons shortening	4	dashes Tabasco sauce
2	tablespoons chili powder		

Season the chicken with salt and pepper and place on a platter. Chill, covered, until ready to grill. Mix the remaining ingredients in a saucepan. Bring to a boil and then reduce the heat. Simmer for 10 minutes, stirring occasionally. Dip the chicken into the sauce and place skin side up on a hot grill. Grill over indirect heat for 1 1/2 to 2 hours, basting with the sauce every 20 minutes. Turn the chicken over and baste with the sauce. Grill for an hour or until the chicken is cooked through, basting every 20 minutes; do not baste during the last 20 minutes of grilling. Discard any remaining sauce.

MAKES 6 TO 8 SERVINGS

Chicken and Dumplings

5	chicken breasts, or	2	chicken bouillon cubes
	1 (2 1/2-pound) chicken, cut up	1/2	teaspoon white pepper
1	teaspoon salt	3	cups self-rising flour
1/2	teaspoon seasoned pepper	1/2	teaspoon poultry seasoning
1/2	teaspoon garlic powder	1/3	cup butter, softened
1/2	teaspoon dried thyme	1	tablespoon bacon drippings
1/4	teaspoon cayenne pepper	1	cup milk

Cover the chicken with water in a large saucepan and bring to a boil. Stir in the salt, seasoned pepper, garlic powder, thyme and cayenne pepper and reduce the heat. Simmer, covered, for 1 hour. Remove the chicken with a slotted spoon to a work surface. Remove the bones and coarsely chop the chicken. Return the chicken to the broth. Stir in the bouillon cubes and white pepper. Cover and return to a simmer. Mix the flour and poultry seasoning in a bowl. Cut in the butter and bacon drippings with a fork until crumbly. Add the milk and stir just until moistened. Roll out the dough on a floured work surface to 1/8-inch thick and cut into 1-inch pieces. Bring the chicken mixture to a boil. Drop the dough into the boiling liquid a few pieces at a time. Stir gently and reduce the heat. Simmer, covered, for 25 minutes, stirring frequently. Let cool slightly before serving to allow the broth to thicken.

MAKES 8 TO 10 SERVINGS

Citrus Chicken

1	teaspoon grated orange zest		1/4	teaspoon salt
1/4	cup orange juice		1/8	teaspoon cayenne pepper
1/2	teaspoon grated lime zest		4	boneless skinless chicken breasts
2	tablespoons fresh lime juice		1	tablespoon olive oil
2	tablespoons chopped fresh thyme		4	cups fresh baby spinach
2	teaspoons minced garlic			

Whisk the orange zest, orange juice, lime zest, lime juice, thyme, garlic, salt and cayenne pepper in a bowl. Remove ¼ cup of the juice mixture to a sealable plastic bag, reserving the remaining juice mixture. Add the chicken to the bag and seal. Let stand for 5 minutes. Whisk the olive oil into the remaining juice mixture. Remove the chicken from the bag and discard the marinade. Heat a large nonstick skillet over medium-high heat and coat with nonstick cooking spray. Add the chicken and cook for 7 minutes per side or until the chicken is cooked through. Arrange equal portions of the spinach on four serving plates and top each with one chicken breast. Spoon equal portions of the reserved juice mixture over each chicken breast.

MAKES 4 SERVINGS

Tandoori Chicken

6	chicken breasts, or 8 to 10 chicken thighs		1	teaspoon ginger
			1	teaspoon paprika
	Juice of 2 lemons or limes		1	teaspoon cinnamon
1	tablespoon curry powder		1	teaspoon turmeric
1	tablespoon red pepper flakes		3/4	cup plain yogurt
1	tablespoon coarse salt			Lemon or lime juice

Remove the skin from the chicken and cut small slits into the chicken. Arrange in a 9×13-inch baking dish. Rub the juice of 2 lemons or limes over the chicken and let stand for 15 minutes. Combine the curry powder, red pepper flakes, salt, ginger, paprika, cinnamon, turmeric and yogurt in a bowl and mix well. Spread over the chicken, coating all sides. Chill, covered, for several hours or overnight. Remove any excess yogurt mixture from the baking dish. Bake at 375 degrees for 45 minutes or until the chicken is cooked through, or grill until the chicken is cooked through. Sprinkle lemon or lime juice over the chicken just before serving.

MAKES 6 SERVINGS

Honey Curry Chicken

1/2	cup honey
1/4	cup yellow mustard
1	tablespoon curry powder
1	teaspoon salt
1/4	cup (1/2 stick) butter, melted
4	chicken breasts

Whisk the honey, mustard, curry powder, salt and butter in a bowl. Pour evenly over the chicken in a 9×13-inch baking dish. Bake at 350 degrees for 45 to 60 minutes or until the chicken is cooked through.

MAKES 4 SERVINGS

Fried Chicken Tenders

2	eggs
1/4	cup milk
4	boneless skinless chicken breasts, cut into strips or bite-size pieces
2	cups all-purpose flour
2	teaspoons salt
2	teaspoons garlic powder
2	teaspoons paprika
1	teaspoon seasoned pepper
1	teaspoon cayenne pepper
	Vegetable oil for frying

Beat the eggs and milk in a large bowl. Add the chicken and stir to coat. Chill for at least 30 minutes. Mix the flour, salt, garlic powder, paprika, seasoned pepper and cayenne pepper in a shallow dish. Remove the chicken from the egg mixture a few pieces at a time and coat in the dry ingredients. Heat oil in a skillet over medium heat until hot. Add the coated chicken a few pieces at a time and fry until golden brown on all sides and the chicken is cooked through. Remove to paper towels to drain. Serve warm.

MAKES 4 TO 6 SERVINGS

Tyson Family Southern Fried Chicken

CHICKEN SEASONING MIX

1	cup salt
1	cup dried thyme
1/4	cup pepper
3 1/2	tablespoons paprika
3	tablespoons garlic powder
2	tablespoons onion powder

CHICKEN

4	eggs, beaten
1/3	cup water
1/2	cup hot red pepper sauce
2	cups self-rising flour
1	teaspoon coarsely ground pepper
1	(2 1/2-pound) chicken, cut up Shortening for frying

SEASONING MIX

Combine the salt, thyme, pepper, paprika, garlic powder and onion powder in a bowl and mix well. Store in an airtight container for up to 6 months.

CHICKEN

Combine the eggs, water and hot sauce in a shallow dish and mix well. Mix the flour and pepper in a shallow dish. Spread enough seasoning mix in a shallow dish to coat all of the chicken. Coat the chicken in the seasoning mix. Dip in the egg mixture and then coat in the flour mixture. Heat shortening in a cast-iron skillet until hot. Fry the chicken for 10 to 12 minutes per side or until the chicken is cooked through. Drain on a wire rack; do not drain on paper towels or the chicken will stick.

MAKES 4 TO 6 SERVINGS

The Tyson family has been a part of Northwest Arkansas' history since 1931, when John Tyson, his wife, and his one-year-old son, Don, moved to Springdale. From poultry deliveries in the 1930s, the company grew to become Tyson Feed and Hatchery in the 1940s. Expansion and acquisitions continued, and in 1966 Don Tyson was named President of Tyson Foods. In 1998 John Tyson became Chairman of the Board. Today, Tyson Foods, Inc. is one of the world's largest processors and marketers of chicken, beef, and pork. Tyson Family Southern Fried Chicken remains a favorite.

Plum Chicken with Couscous

You may use four chickens, halved, instead of chicken breasts or thighs.

7 1/2	pounds boneless chicken breasts and/or thighs
1/2	teaspoon salt
1/2	teaspoon pepper
5	garlic cloves, minced
1/4	cup dried oregano
1	tablespoon dried tarragon
1/2	cup red wine vinegar
1/2	cup olive oil
1	cup pitted green olives
1/2	cup capers
2	cups pitted prunes (dried plums)
1	cup lightly packed brown sugar
1	cup white wine
2	(10-ounce) packages couscous
1/2	cup flat-leaf parsley
1/2	cup pine nuts

Arrange the chicken in a single layer in an 11×13-inch baking dish. Sprinkle the salt, pepper, garlic, oregano and tarragon over the chicken. Pour the wine vinegar and olive oil over the chicken. Sprinkle the olives, capers and prunes over the chicken. Chill, covered with plastic wrap, overnight. Sprinkle the brown sugar over the chicken and pour the wine over the top. Bake at 350 degrees for 50 to 60 minutes or until the chicken is cooked through, basting frequently with the pan juices. Prepare the couscous according to the package directions. Spread the couscous over a serving platter. Remove the chicken, olives, capers and prunes with a slotted spoon from the baking dish and arrange over the couscous. Sprinkle with the parsley and pine nuts. Pour the pan juices into a gravy boat and serve on the side.

MAKES 12 TO 14 SERVINGS

PHOTO ON PAGE 109

Helen R. Walton's Christmas Quail

From the recipe files of Helen R. Walton:
"I grew up in a family where quail was our favorite dish, and we always had gravy on rice or mashed potatoes when we had it. My father was an avid quail hunter, so my mother became an expert on cooking quail to perfection. This is her recipe."

6	quail, skin removed	2	cups (or more) milk
	Salt		Salt and pepper to taste
	All-purpose flour for coating		Hot cooked rice or mashed
	Vegetable oil for frying		cooked potatoes
3	tablespoons all-purpose flour		

Rinse the quail and pat dry. Season all sides of the quail with salt. Add flour to a paper bag and add the quail one at a time. Shake the bag to coat the quail with flour. Heat 2½ inches of oil in a heavy skillet until hot. Add the quail breast side down. Fry for 10 minutes or until the quail are golden brown and cooked through, turning once during frying. Remove the quail to paper towels to drain and keep warm. Remove and discard all but 3 tablespoons of oil from the skillet. Stir 3 tablespoons flour into the skillet. Cook over medium heat until the mixture is light brown, stirring constantly. Stir in the milk gradually. Cook until thickened, stirring constantly. Add additional milk if needed to reach the desired consistency. Season with salt and pepper. Serve hot with rice or mashed potatoes.

MAKES 3 SERVINGS

Courtesy of the Walton family

The story of American retail cannot be told without Sam Walton, pictured here with wife Helen, and Wal-Mart, the world's largest retailer. Walton's vision for a "better life for all" included his company's and his family's contributions beyond the retail realm as generous contributors to communities around the world. The first Wal-Mart store opened in Rogers in 1962. The Wal-Mart Visitors Center in Bentonville is located in the original Walton's 5 & 10 on the historic Bentonville Square.

Halibut Parmesan

3	tablespoons all-purpose flour	3	tablespoons milk
3	tablespoons yellow cornmeal	2¹/₂	pounds halibut fillets
¹/₂	teaspoon garlic salt	3	tablespoons butter, melted
¹/₂	teaspoon dry mustard	1	teaspoon paprika
¹/₄	teaspoon dried rosemary	¹/₂	cup (2 ounces) shredded
¹/₄	teaspoon pepper		Parmesan cheese

Mix the flour, cornmeal, garlic salt, dry mustard, rosemary and pepper in a shallow dish. Pour the milk into a bowl. Dip the halibut into the milk and then coat on all sides in the flour mixture. Arrange the halibut in a single layer in a 9×13-inch baking dish. Drizzle the butter evenly over the fish. Sprinkle with half the paprika and half the cheese. Bake at 350 degrees for 5 to 7 minutes. Turn the fish over and sprinkle with the remaining paprika and cheese. Bake for 5 to 10 minutes longer or until the fish flakes easily.

MAKES 4 SERVINGS

Grilled Feta Shrimp

6	tablespoons olive oil	12	deveined peeled large shrimp
¹/₄	cup fresh lime juice		with tails
3	large garlic cloves, pressed	2	(¹/₂-inch) red onion slices
1	tablespoon chopped cilantro	2	ounces crumbled feta cheese
		1¹/₂	tablespoons chopped cilantro

Combine the olive oil, lime juice, garlic and 1 tablespoon cilantro in a bowl and mix well. Add the shrimp and toss to coat. Let stand for 10 minutes. Remove the shrimp from the marinade, reserving the marinade. Thread six shrimp on each of two metal or bamboo skewers. Thread the onion slices on one skewer. Spoon a small amount of the marinade over the shrimp and onions. Grill the onions over hot coals for 3 minutes per side or until tender. Remove the onions from the skewers and chop coarsely. Add the shrimp to the grill and cook for 2 minutes per side or until the shrimp turn pink. Remove to two serving plates. Pour the reserved marinade into a saucepan and bring to a boil. Stir in the chopped onions, cheese and 1¹/₂ tablespoons cilantro. Spoon over the shrimp.

MAKES 2 SERVINGS

Cream Cheese Shrimp

2	pounds shrimp, peeled and deveined
	Juice of 2 limes
1/2	cup (1 stick) butter
6	ounces cream cheese
2	ounces crumbled blue cheese
	Hot cooked rice or pasta

Arrange the shrimp in a single layer in a 9×13-inch baking dish. Sprinkle with the lime juice. Combine the butter, cream cheese and blue cheese in a heavy saucepan. Cook until melted, stirring frequently. Pour evenly over the shrimp. Bake at 400 degrees for 20 minutes or until the shrimp turn pink. Serve over rice or pasta.

MAKES 4 TO 6 SERVINGS

> The railroad played an important role in the history of the city of Rogers. The route of the Frisco Railroad line established a business district of a community that took its name from the general manager of the line, Captain C.W. Rogers. Commemorating the historical significance of the railroad is the Frisco Caboose located in downtown Rogers near the tracks, which are still used today by the Arkansas and Missouri Railroad. Given to the city in 1981 by the Frisco Railroad, the caboose stands as a permanent reminder of the city's railroad roots.

Shrimp Scampi

¼	cup chopped green onions
2	tablespoons minced garlic
¾	cup (1½ sticks) butter
2	pounds shrimp, peeled and deveined
	Hot cooked linguine
½	cup dry white wine
3	tablespoons lemon juice
1	tablespoon chopped parsley
	Salt and pepper to taste

Sauté the green onions and garlic in the butter in a skillet until tender. Add the shrimp and sauté for 5 minutes or until the shrimp turn pink. Remove the shrimp with a slotted spoon to a bed of linguine on a platter and keep warm. Add the wine, lemon juice, parsley, salt and pepper to the skillet. Simmer for 5 minutes, stirring frequently. Pour over the shrimp.

MAKES 4 SERVINGS

Wonderful Peppered Shrimp

2½	pounds unpeeled shrimp, rinsed
1¼	cups Italian salad dressing
	Juice of 2 lemons
1	cup (2 sticks) butter, melted
1	tablespoon pepper

Arrange the shrimp in a single layer in a 9×13-inch baking dish. Combine the salad dressing, lemon juice and butter in a bowl and mix well. Pour evenly over the shrimp. Sprinkle the pepper evenly over the top. Bake at 350 degrees for 25 to 30 minutes or until the shrimp turn pink; do not overcook.

MAKES 4 TO 6 SERVINGS

Pat Walker's Chicken Spaghetti

8	ounces spaghetti
	Chicken stock
3/4	cup chopped onion
3/4	cup chopped celery
1/2	cup chopped bell pepper
1/2	cup (1 stick) butter
4 to	6 chicken breasts, cooked,
	boned and chopped
1	(4-ounce) can sliced mushrooms
1	(10-ounce) can condensed tomato soup
1	(10-ounce) can condensed cream of
	mushroom soup
	Salt and pepper to taste
1	teaspoon chili powder
2	cups (8 ounces) shredded Colby cheese

Cook the spaghetti in stock in a saucepan until al dente. Drain, reserving 2 to 3 cups of the stock. Sauté the onion, celery and bell pepper in the butter in a large saucepan until tender. Stir in the chicken, mushrooms, tomato soup, mushroom soup, salt, pepper and chili powder. Stir in the reserved stock to reach the desired consistency. Spoon into a 9×13-inch baking dish and sprinkle with the cheese. Bake at 350 degrees for 45 to 60 minutes or until bubbly. You may substitute one whole chicken for the chicken breasts if desired.

MAKES 10 TO 12 SERVINGS

> For a romantic votive, remove the center of a fully bloomed rose, trim the bottom flat, and insert a tealight.

Robin George's Chicken Spaghetti

2	hens
2	large onions, chopped
2	green bell peppers, chopped
1	cup (2 sticks) butter
32	ounces spaghetti
1	(14-ounce) can tomatoes with green chiles
1	(4-ounce) jar pimentos
32	ounces Velveeta cheese, chopped
1	cup chopped mushrooms

Cover the chickens with water in a stockpot. Bring to a boil and reduce the heat. Simmer until the chickens are cooked through. Remove with a slotted spoon to a work surface and let cool, reserving the broth. Remove the skin and bones and cut the chicken into bite-size pieces. Sauté the onions and bell pepper in the butter in a skillet over low heat for 15 minutes, stirring occasionally. Bring the reserved broth to a boil in the stockpot. Add the spaghetti and cook until al dente; do not drain. Add the chicken, onion mixture, tomatoes with green chiles, pimentos, cheese and mushrooms and mix well. Spoon into two large baking dishes. Bake at 350 degrees for 30 minutes. This recipe freezes well.

MAKES 20 TO 24 SERVINGS

George's, Inc. is a family-owned company that began in the late 1920s. Today it is a fully integrated poultry operation headquartered in Springdale and is one of the top poultry and egg producers in the country. Begun by C. L. George and his sons, Luther and Gene, the legacy was passed to Gene George in 1969 when C. L. and Luther George died within weeks of each other. In 1980 Gene George turned over the presidency of the company to his son, Gary George. The fourth generation began with the addition of Gary and Robin George's twin sons, Charles and Carl, to the executive team upon their graduation from the University of Arkansas.

Company's Coming White Lasagna

1/2	cup (1 stick) butter	2	tablespoons dry white wine
1/2	cup all-purpose flour	8	ounces sliced mushrooms
4	cups milk	9	ounces baby spinach
	Salt and pepper to taste	1 1/2	teaspoons minced garlic
1	teaspoon dried oregano	1	teaspoon Tabasco sauce
1	teaspoon dried rosemary	15	ounces whole milk
1/2	teaspoon dried marjoram		ricotta cheese
1/2	teaspoon dried thyme	1	egg
3	tablespoons butter	1 1/2	teaspoons dried basil
5	boneless skinless chicken	15	no-boil lasagna noodles
	breasts, cut into 1/2-inch strips	1/2	cup (2 ounces) freshly grated
1 1/2	teaspoons minced garlic		Parmesan cheese

Melt 1/2 cup butter in a saucepan over medium-low heat. Stir in the flour. Cook for 3 minutes, stirring constantly. Whisk in the milk in a steady stream. Bring to a boil, whisking constantly. Season with salt and pepper. Simmer over low heat for 10 to 12 minutes, whisking occasionally. Remove to a bowl and press a buttered sheet of waxed paper over the surface.

Crumble the oregano, rosemary, marjoram and thyme into a bowl and mix well. Melt 3 tablespoons butter in a large skillet over medium heat. Add the chicken, 1 1/2 teaspoons garlic and half the herb mixture and sauté for 5 minutes or until the chicken is cooked through. Remove the chicken with a slotted spoon to a large bowl.

Add the wine to the skillet and bring to a boil. Stir in the mushrooms and spinach. Cook, covered, until the spinach is wilted. Stir in 1 1/2 teaspoons garlic, the remaining herb mixture and the Tabasco sauce and season with salt and pepper. Cook until the liquid has evaporated, stirring occasionally. Add to the chicken mixture and mix well.

Reserve 1 cup of the white sauce and add the remaining white sauce to the chicken mixture. Season with salt and pepper and mix well. Whisk the ricotta cheese, egg and basil in a bowl and season with salt and pepper.

Spread 1/2 cup of the reserved white sauce over the bottom of a buttered 9x13-inch baking dish. Arrange three lasagna noodles over the sauce, making certain the noodles do not touch. Spread half the chicken mixture over the noodles and top with three lasagna noodles. Spread half the ricotta cheese mixture over the noodles and top with three lasagna noodles. Continue layering the chicken mixture, noodles and ricotta mixture, ending with noodles. Spread the remaining white sauce over the noodles and sprinkle with the Parmesan cheese. Bake at 350 degrees for 45 minutes.

MAKES 12 TO 15 SERVINGS

Rigatoni

1½	pounds ground beef	1	(6-ounce) can tomato paste
½	cup chopped onion	½	teaspoon sugar
1	garlic clove, minced	8	ounces rigatoni, cooked and drained
1	tablespoon parsley		
1	teaspoon pepper	1	cup (4 ounces) shredded mozzarella cheese
½	teaspoon oregano		
¼	teaspoon basil	¼	cup (1 ounce) grated Parmesan cheese
2	(14-ounce) cans whole tomatoes		

Brown the ground beef with the onion and garlic in a skillet, stirring until the ground beef is crumbly; drain. Stir in the parsley, pepper, oregano, basil, tomatoes, tomato paste and sugar. Bring to a boil and then reduce the heat. Simmer for 30 minutes. Remove to a large bowl. Add the pasta, mozzarella cheese and Parmesan cheese and mix well. Spoon into a 3-quart baking dish. Bake, covered, at 350 degrees for 15 to 20 minutes or until the cheese is melted.

MAKES 8 SERVINGS

Pistachio Pesto Pasta

1	cup (4 ounces) freshly grated Parmesan cheese	½	teaspoon salt
		½	teaspoon pepper
½	cup crushed roasted pistachios	1	tablespoon olive oil
5	garlic cloves, minced	4	boneless chicken breasts, chopped
½	cup olive oil		
1	cup packed basil leaves, stems removed	1	tablespoon balsamic vinegar
		16	ounces farfalle, cooked and drained
¼	cup packed parsley sprigs, stems removed		

Process the cheese, pistachios, garlic, ½ cup olive oil, the basil, parsley, salt and pepper in a food processor to form a thick paste. Sauté the chicken in 1 tablespoon olive oil and the balsamic vinegar in a large skillet until the chicken is cooked through. Add ½ cup of the pesto and the pasta to the skillet and mix well. Freeze the unused pesto for another use.

MAKES 4 TO 8 SERVINGS

Artichoke Chicken Pasta

4	boneless skinless chicken breasts, cut into 1-inch pieces	8	ounces sliced mushrooms
1/2	teaspoon salt	1 to	2 tablespoons chopped fresh rosemary
1	teaspoon freshly ground pepper	1/4	cup (1/2 stick) butter
1/4	cup (1/2 stick) butter	1/3	cup dry white wine
1	small sweet onion, sliced	2	cups heavy cream
2	garlic cloves, crushed	1	(9-ounce) package refrigerator fettuccini, cooked
6	plum tomatoes, seeded and chopped	3/4	cup (3 ounces) freshly grated Parmesan cheese
1	(12-ounce) jar marinated artichoke heart quarters, drained		

Sprinkle the chicken with the salt and pepper. Melt 1/4 cup butter in a large heavy saucepan over medium-high heat. Add the chicken and sauté for 5 minutes or until light brown and cooked through. Remove the chicken with a slotted spoon to a bowl. Add the onion, garlic, tomatoes, artichokes, mushrooms and rosemary to the saucepan and sauté for 10 minutes or until the vegetables are tender; drain. Add the cooked vegetables to the chicken. Add 1/4 cup butter, the wine and cream to the saucepan. Cook over medium heat for 10 minutes or until thickened, stirring constantly. Add the chicken mixture, pasta and cheese and toss gently to mix.

MAKES 4 SERVINGS

Sun-Dried Tomato Pesto

1	cup sun-dried tomatoes	3/4	cup walnuts
1	cup (4 ounces) grated Romano cheese	1 1/2	teaspoons fresh parsley or dried parsley flakes
1/2	cup olive oil	1	tablespoon minced garlic
1/2	cup tomato sauce		Hot cooked pasta

Combine the tomatoes, cheese, olive oil, tomato sauce, walnuts, parsley and garlic in a food processor fitted with a steel blade. Process until coarsely chopped. Scrape down the side and process until smooth. Serve over pasta.

MAKES 4 SERVINGS

Hot Sausage Pasta

1	pound hot Italian pork sausage links, casings removed
3	tablespoons butter
1	teaspoon dried rosemary
3	tablespoons water
1	(28-ounce) can diced tomatoes
	Red pepper flakes to taste
	Salt to taste
3/4	cup heavy cream
16	ounces pasta shells, cooked and drained
1/2	cup (2 ounces) shredded Parmesan cheese

Cover the sausage with water in a large skillet. Boil for 3 to 4 minutes or until cooked through; drain. Cut the sausage into round slices. Melt the butter in the skillet. Sauté the sausage in the butter until light brown. Stir in the rosemary, 3 tablespoons water and the tomatoes. Cook for 7 to 10 minutes or until slightly thickened, stirring frequently. Season with red pepper flakes and salt. Stir in the cream gradually and cook until the cream is reduced by half and the sauce is creamy, stirring frequently. Combine the sausage mixture with the pasta in a large bowl and toss to mix. Sprinkle with the cheese and serve.

MAKES 6 SERVINGS

Meaty Spaghetti Sauce

1 1/2	pounds lean ground beef
1	onion, chopped
1	(15-ounce) can diced tomatoes
1	(8-ounce) can tomato paste
1	tablespoon oregano
1	teaspoon celery salt
1	teaspoon garlic salt
3 to	5 bay leaves
	Salt and pepper to taste
1	cup water

Brown the ground beef in a skillet, stirring until crumbly; drain. Combine the onion, tomatoes, tomato paste, oregano, celery salt, garlic salt, bay leaves, salt, pepper and water and in a large saucepan. Stir in the ground beef. Cook over low heat for 1 1/2 hours, stirring occasionally. Remove the bay leaves.

MAKES 8 SERVINGS

Fettuccine Alfredo

You may add cooked shrimp or crab meat to this recipe.

1/4	cup (1/2 stick) butter
1/2	cup half-and-half
8	ounces refrigerator fettuccine, cooked
1/2	cup half-and-half
3/4	cup (3 ounces) freshly grated Parmesan cheese
	Pepper to taste

Melt the butter in a saucepan and stir in 1/2 cup half-and-half. Simmer for 1 minute. Add the pasta and toss to mix. Add 1/2 cup half-and-half, the cheese and pepper and toss to mix. Serve immediately.

MAKES 2 SERVINGS

For a dinner party, create unique place card or menu holders from items found around the house and in your pantry. Use seashells or starfish for a summer party. Slip a card under the petal of an artichoke for an elegant touch. Affix cards to the stems of small pumpkins or gourds for a festive fall table.

Weekend Navy Beans and Ham

1	pound navy beans, sorted and rinsed
3	tablespoons olive oil
4	ham hocks, scored
1	cup minced yellow onion
1/4	cup finely chopped celery
1/4	cup finely chopped green bell pepper
1/2	teaspoon crushed red pepper flakes
1/4	teaspoon dried oregano
1/8	teaspoon dried thyme
1	bay leaf
1	tablespoon minced garlic
8	cups chicken broth
1/2	teaspoon salt
1/4	cup minced fresh parsley
1/3	cup minced green onions

Cover the beans with water. Let soak overnight; drain. Heat the olive oil in a large stockpot over medium heat. Add the ham hocks, yellow onion, celery, bell pepper, red pepper flakes, oregano, thyme and bay leaf and sauté for 5 to 7 minutes or until the vegetables are tender. Add the garlic and sauté for 1 minute. Add the broth and bring to a boil over high heat. Reduce the heat. Simmer, covered, for 1 1/2 hours, stirring occasionally. Stir in the navy beans and simmer for 45 to 60 minutes or until the beans are almost tender and the ham hocks are very tender. Stir in the salt and simmer for 20 to 30 minutes or until the beans are very tender and the ham hocks are beginning to fall apart. Remove the bay leaf. Remove the meat from the ham hocks and return the meat to the stockpot, if desired. Ladle into serving bowls and sprinkle with the parsley and green onions.

MAKES 6 SERVINGS

Football Season Muffulettas

You may use round sandwich buns instead of a bread loaf to make individual muffulettas.

1½   cups pimento-stuffed olives, drained and finely chopped
1   cup pitted black olives, drained and finely chopped
1   rib celery, finely chopped
6   garlic cloves, minced
⅓   cup olive oil
⅓   cup vinegar
2 to   3 tablespoons butter, softened
1 or   2 loaves fresh bread, cut into halves horizontally
1   teaspoon Italian seasoning
4   ounces ham, thinly sliced
4   ounces turkey, thinly sliced
4   ounces Genoa salami, thinly sliced
6   slices provolone cheese
6   slices mozzarella cheese
½   cup (2 ounces) shredded Cheddar cheese

Combine the pimento-stuffed olives, black olives, celery, garlic, olive oil and vinegar in a bowl and mix well. Chill, covered, for 8 hours or overnight. Spread the butter over half of each loaf and sprinkle evenly with the Italian seasoning. Top the Italian seasoning with the olive mixture. Layer the ham, turkey, salami, provolone cheese, mozzarella cheese and Cheddar cheese over the olive mixture. Top with the remaining bread halves and wrap tightly in foil. Bake at 350 degrees for 20 to 30 minutes or until the cheese is melted. Remove the foil and place the loaf on a cutting board. Slice the loaf into individual sandwiches. Store any remaining olive mixture in the refrigerator for up to 1 week.

MAKES 6 TO 8 SERVINGS

ON THE SIDE

Vegetables and
Side Dishes

Roasted Asparagus with Parmesan

2½   pounds fresh asparagus, trimmed
3   tablespoons olive oil
¾   teaspoon kosher salt or freshly ground salt
¼   teaspoon freshly ground pepper
¼   cup (1 ounce) freshly grated Parmesan cheese

Arrange the asparagus on an ungreased baking sheet in a single layer. Drizzle with the olive oil and sprinkle with the salt and pepper. Bake at 350 degrees for 15 to 18 minutes or until tender. Sprinkle the cheese over the asparagus and bake for 1 minute longer.

MAKES 4 TO 6 SERVINGS

Busy Baked Beans

3   (28-ounce) cans vegetarian beans, drained
¾   cup molasses
½   cup ketchup
¼   cup (½ stick) butter
1   (6-ounce) package frozen chopped onions
1   large green bell pepper, chopped
3   ribs celery with leaves, chopped
      Salt and pepper to taste
1   tablespoon liquid smoke
½   cup packed brown sugar
1   teaspoon garlic powder

Warm the beans in a large skillet over low heat. Stir in the molasses and ketchup. Melt the butter in a skillet. Add the onions, bell pepper and celery and sauté until tender. Season with salt and pepper. Add to the beans and mix well. Stir in the liquid smoke, brown sugar and garlic powder. Spoon into a 2-quart or 9×13-inch baking dish. Bake at 300 degrees for 30 minutes or until bubbly.

MAKES 12 SERVINGS

Broccoli with Browned Garlic

4	*broccoli crowns, cut into florets*
1/2	*cup (1 stick) butter*
1/2	*cup olive oil*
2	*garlic bulbs*

Steam the broccoli over a saucepan of simmering water until tender-crisp. Remove the broccoli to a bowl and keep warm. Heat the butter and olive oil in a skillet over medium heat. Add the garlic cloves and sauté until golden brown and soft; do not burn. Pour over the broccoli and toss to mix. Serve warm.

MAKES 4 SERVINGS

Don't be afraid to mix china, glassware, and linen patterns. Using serving containers of different sizes, shapes, colors, and materials adds interest.

Celebration Celery

4   cups (1/2-inch diagonal slices) celery
     Salt to taste
1/4 cup chopped pimentos
1   (5-ounce) can water chestnuts, thinly sliced
1   (10-ounce) can condensed cream of chicken soup
2   tablespoons butter
1   slice bread, cut into small cubes
1/4 cup blanched almonds, thinly sliced

Cook the celery in a small amount of boiling salted water in a saucepan for 8 minutes or until tender-crisp; drain. Remove the celery to a 2-quart baking dish. Add the pimentos, water chestnuts and soup and mix carefully. Melt the butter in a saucepan. Add the bread cubes and almonds and toss to mix. Spoon the bread cubes over the celery mixture and bake at 350 degrees for 35 minutes or until golden brown.

MAKES 6 OR 7 SERVINGS

Green Chile and Corn Casserole

2   tablespoons butter
1/4 cup milk
8   ounces cream cheese
2   (11-ounce) cans white Shoe Peg corn, drained
1   (4-ounce) can green chiles
1/8 teaspoon salt
1/4 teaspoon pepper
1/8 teaspoon garlic salt
2   drops of Tabasco sauce

Melt the butter in a saucepan. Add the milk and cream cheese. Cook until the cream cheese is melted, stirring constantly. Add the corn, green chiles, salt, pepper, garlic salt and Tabasco sauce and mix well. Spoon into a 2-quart baking dish and bake at 350 degrees for 30 minutes.

MAKES 6 SERVINGS

Linda Allen Brown's Green Beans

3/4	cup packed brown sugar
1	teaspoon garlic powder
5	teaspoons soy sauce
1/2	cup (1 stick) butter, melted
	Salt and pepper to taste
5	cans Allen's whole green beans, drained
10	slices bacon

Combine the brown sugar, garlic powder, soy sauce, butter, salt and pepper in a bowl and mix well. Pour over the beans in a shallow bowl. Chill, covered, overnight. Cook the bacon in a skillet just until the edges curl; remove to paper towels to drain. Remove the beans from the marinade and divide into ten bundles; discard the marinade. Wrap one bacon slice around each bean bundle and arrange in a 9×13-inch baking pan. Bake at 375 degrees for 45 minutes.

MAKES 10 SERVINGS

Allen Canning Co. is one of the largest privately held vegetable canning companies in the country. In 1926, Earl Allen purchased the canning company near Siloam Springs where he had been working. For three generations, Allen Canning has grown and flourished and now offers canned vegetables under thirteen different brand names. Linda Allen Brown is the granddaughter of the Allen Canning Co. founder. She shared one of her favorite Allen green bean recipes.

Dilled Green Beans

This recipe may easily be doubled by adding a second layer of all the ingredients.

2	(15-ounce) cans cut green beans, drained
3	green onions, chopped
2	tablespoons white vinegar
	Pepper to taste
1/3	cup sour cream
1/3	cup mayonnaise
1	rounded teaspoon dill weed

Place the beans in a serving bowl and top evenly with the green onions. Drizzle with the vinegar and season with pepper. Mix the sour cream and mayonnaise in a bowl and spread over the top. Sprinkle with the dill weed. Chill, covered, overnight.

MAKES 6 SERVINGS

Souped-Up Green Beans

1/2	cup (1 stick) butter, cut into pieces
3	tablespoons all-purpose flour
1	(10-ounce) can condensed cream of mushroom soup
8	ounces Velveeta cheese, cut into cubes
1 1/2	teaspoons minced onion
2	teaspoons Worcestershire sauce
4	dashes of Tabasco sauce
4	(15-ounce) cans cut green beans, drained

Mix the butter, flour, soup, cheese, onion, Worcestershire sauce and Tabasco sauce in a microwave-safe bowl. Microwave on High until the cheese and butter are melted, stirring frequently. Spread the beans into a 9×13-inch baking dish. Pour the cheese sauce over the beans and mix gently. Bake at 350 degrees for 45 to 60 minutes.

MAKES 6 TO 8 SERVINGS

Stuffed Portobello Mushrooms

1	(6-ounce) package long grain and wild rice mix
6	portobello mushrooms, stems removed
12	ounces cream cheese, softened
2	tablespoons pesto
	Salt to taste
6	(1/2-inch-thick) tomato slices
1/2	cup (2 ounces) shredded Parmesan cheese
6	basil leaves

Prepare the rice according to the package directions. Arrange the mushroom caps, top side down, in a foil-lined 10×15-inch baking pan. Combine the cream cheese, pesto and salt in a bowl and mix well. Spread equal portions of the pesto mixture into the mushroom caps. Spoon equal portions of the rice over the pesto mixture. Top each with one tomato slice and sprinkle with the Parmesan cheese. Bake at 400 degrees for 20 minutes. Top each mushroom with a basil leaf and serve.

MAKES 6 SERVINGS

The holiday season is illuminated in Northwest Arkansas by the annual Lights of the Ozarks event. Thousands of twinkling lights attract many visitors. This event features a Christmas parade, local choir events, and miles of lights on trees and buildings.

Helen R. Walton's Sweet Onion Pie Supreme

3   *cups thinly sliced Vidalia onions*
3   *tablespoons butter*
1   *baked (9-inch) pie shell*
3   *tablespoons all-purpose flour*
1   *teaspoon salt*
1/4   *cup sour cream*
1/2   *cup milk*
1 1/4 *cups sour cream*
2   *eggs, well beaten*
     Crumbled crisp-cooked bacon for garnish
     Sautéed onion slices for garnish

Sauté the onions in the butter until golden brown and spoon into the pie shell. Combine the flour, salt and 1/4 cup sour cream in a bowl and mix well. Combine the milk and 1 1/4 cups sour cream in a bowl and mix well. Add the eggs and flour mixture and mix well. Pour over the onions in the pie shell. Bake at 325 degrees for 45 minutes or until the center is set. Remove to a wire rack to cool. Garnish with bacon and sautéed onion.

MAKES 6 TO 8 SERVINGS

Potato Hash with Rosemary

1   *large russet potato, peeled and chopped*
1   *large sweet potato, peeled and chopped*
1/4   *cup chopped onion*
2   *garlic cloves, minced*
2   *tablespoons olive oil*
1   *tablespoon chopped fresh rosemary*
1/2   *teaspoon salt*
1/2   *teaspoon freshly ground pepper*
     Fresh rosemary sprigs for garnish

Combine the russet potato, sweet potato, onion, garlic, olive oil, 1 tablespoon rosemary, the salt and pepper in a bowl and mix well. Spread into a lightly greased nonstick skillet. Cook, covered, over medium-low heat for 25 minutes or until the potatoes are tender, stirring occasionally. Garnish with rosemary sprigs.

MAKES 4 SERVINGS

Rosemary Potatoes

6	*tablespoons butter*
1	*onion, sliced*
2	*garlic cloves, minced*
1	*teaspoon Creole seasoning*
1	*tablespoon dried rosemary*
1/2	*teaspoon pepper*
5	*russet potatoes, peeled and sliced*
1/2	*cup (2 ounces) grated Parmesan, asiago cheese or shredded Cheddar cheese*

Melt the butter in a skillet. Add the onion and sauté over medium-high heat for 5 minutes or until translucent. Reduce the heat to medium. Add the garlic, Creole seasoning, rosemary and pepper and sauté for 2 minutes. Spread half the potatoes in a 2-quart baking dish. Add half the onion mixture and stir to coat. Add the remaining potatoes and remaining onion mixture and stir to coat. Bake, covered, at 375 degrees for 45 minutes. Sprinkle with the cheese. Bake, uncovered, for 15 minutes longer or until the cheese is melted.

MAKES 12 SERVINGS

PHOTO ON PAGE 131

Chantilly Potatoes

6	*potatoes, peeled, boiled and drained*
1/2	*cup milk*
3	*tablespoons butter*
	Salt and pepper to taste
1/2	*cup heavy whipping cream, whipped*
1	*teaspoon paprika*
	Chopped fresh chives for garnish

Beat the potatoes in a mixing bowl until mashed. Add the milk, butter, salt and pepper and beat until smooth. Spoon into a greased 2-quart baking dish. Spread the whipped cream over the top and sprinkle with the paprika. Bake at 350 degrees for 30 minutes or until light brown. Garnish with chopped chives.

MAKES 6 SERVINGS

Internationally renowned architect E. Fay Jones, FAIA (1921–2004), lived, worked, and taught in Fayetteville. Jones served as a fellow at mentor Frank Lloyd Wright's Taliesin West in 1953. Mr. Jones hosted Wright's visit in 1958 to the University of Arkansas. Fay Jones's legacy is one of lasting architecture in Northwest Arkansas and throughout the world. Thorncrown Chapel in Eureka Springs, the Fulbright Peace Fountain on the university campus, and the Mildred B. Cooper Memorial Chapel in Bella Vista are among his many designs. The Buckley Residence, designed in 1967, is an example of Jones's ability to turn the practical into art.

Smoked Gouda Mashed Potatoes

3   *pounds potatoes, peeled and chopped*
1   *teaspoon salt*
6   *tablespoons unsalted butter*
3/4 *cup heavy cream*
3   *cups (12 ounces) shredded smoked Gouda cheese*
     Salt and freshly ground white pepper to taste

Cover the potatoes and 1 teaspoon salt with water in a saucepan. Bring to a boil over medium heat and cook for 15 to 20 minutes or until tender; drain. Add the butter, cream and cheese and mash well. Season to taste with salt and white pepper.

MAKES 6 SERVINGS

Helen R. Walton's Potato Casserole

1   *(32-ounce) package frozen hash brown potatoes*
1/4 *cup (1/2 stick) butter, melted*
2   *cups sour cream*
1   *(10-ounce) can condensed cream of chicken soup*
10 *ounces cheese, shredded*
1/2 *cup chopped onion*
     Salt and pepper to taste
1   *cup cornflakes or bran flake cereal*
2   *tablespoons butter, melted*

Combine the potatoes, 1/4 cup butter, the sour cream, soup, cheese, onion, salt and pepper in a bowl and mix well. Spoon into a buttered 3-quart baking dish or spread into 9×13-inch baking dish. Combine the cornflakes and 2 tablespoons butter in a bowl and mix well. Sprinkle over the potatoes. Bake at 350 degrees for 45 minutes.

MAKES 16 SERVINGS

Baked Spinach

This dish can be made one day ahead and chilled until ready to bake.

1/2	cup (1 stick) unsalted butter
3	tablespoons all-purpose flour
1/2	onion, chopped
3	(10-ounce) packages frozen chopped spinach, thawed and drained
3	eggs, lightly beaten
2	cups small curd cottage cheese
1 1/2	cups (6 ounces) shredded Cheddar cheese or Colby cheese
	Salt and freshly ground pepper to taste

Melt the butter in a 7×11-inch baking dish in a 350-degree oven. Maintain the oven temperature. Add the flour and onion and mix well. Combine the spinach, eggs, cottage cheese, Cheddar cheese, salt and pepper in a bowl and mix well. Add to the onion mixture in the baking dish and mix well; spread evenly in the baking dish. Bake for 1 hour.

MAKES 6 SERVINGS

Fill half a watermelon with ice and chill bottled beverages for a summer party.

Sweet Potato Puff with Pecan Crumble

3	cups mashed cooked sweet potatoes
1¾	cups granulated sugar
3	tablespoons butter, melted
½	cup milk
1	teaspoon salt
2	eggs, well beaten
½	teaspoon vanilla extract
1	cup packed brown sugar
½	cup self-rising flour
1	cup chopped pecans
3	tablespoons butter, melted

Combine the sweet potatoes, granulated sugar, 3 tablespoons butter, the milk and salt in a mixing bowl. Beat at high speed for 2 to 3 minutes, scraping the side of the bowl frequently. Add the eggs and beat at high speed for 3 to 4 minutes. Stir in the vanilla. Pour into a well-greased 8- or 9-inch baking dish. Combine the brown sugar, flour, pecans and 3 tablespoons butter in a bowl and mix until crumbly. Sprinkle evenly over the sweet potato mixture. Bake at 350 degrees for 35 minutes.

MAKES 10 SERVINGS

Holiday Sweet Potato Casserole

SWEET POTATO CASSEROLE

2	(15-ounce) cans sweet potatoes, drained
1	tablespoon grated orange zest
2/3	cup orange juice
5	tablespoons Grand Marnier
1	teaspoon ginger
1/4	cup packed light brown sugar
2	teaspoons salt
	Dash of pepper
1/4	cup (1/2 stick) butter, melted
1	egg, lightly beaten

TOPPING

1/2	cup (1 stick) butter, melted
2/3	cup packed light brown sugar
1	teaspoon cinnamon
1	cup chopped pecans

CASSEROLE

Beat the sweet potatoes in a mixing bowl until smooth. Beat in the orange zest, orange juice, liqueur, ginger, brown sugar, salt, pepper, butter and egg. Pour into a buttered 9×13-inch baking dish.

TOPPING

Combine the butter, brown sugar, cinnamon and pecans in a bowl and mix well. Sprinkle evenly over the sweet potato mixture. Let stand for 1 hour. Bake at 350 degrees for 45 to 60 minutes or until the filling is set and the topping is golden.

MAKES 12 SERVINGS

Thyme-Scented Savory Sweet Potato Soufflé

6	large sweet potatoes, peeled and sliced
	Salt and white pepper to taste
1/4	cup (1/2 stick) butter, softened
3	eggs, beaten
1/4	cup heavy cream
1	teaspoon sage
1/2	teaspoon dried thyme

Boil the sweet potatoes in water to cover in a saucepan until tender; drain. Remove the sweet potatoes to a mixing bowl. Add the salt, white pepper, butter, eggs, cream, sage and thyme and beat until light and fluffy. Pour into a buttered 2-quart baking dish. Bake at 350 degrees for 30 to 40 minutes or until slightly puffed and golden brown.

MAKES 8 TO 10 SERVINGS

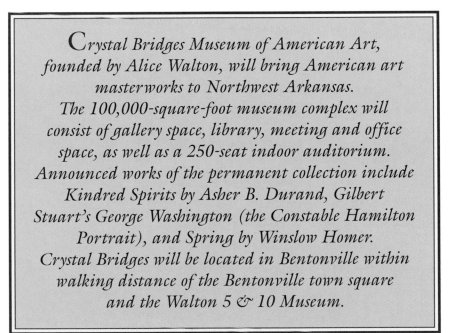

Crystal Bridges Museum of American Art, founded by Alice Walton, will bring American art masterworks to Northwest Arkansas.
The 100,000-square-foot museum complex will consist of gallery space, library, meeting and office space, as well as a 250-seat indoor auditorium.
Announced works of the permanent collection include Kindred Spirits by Asher B. Durand, Gilbert Stuart's George Washington (the Constable Hamilton Portrait), and Spring by Winslow Homer.
Crystal Bridges will be located in Bentonville within walking distance of the Bentonville town square and the Walton 5 & 10 Museum.

Roasted Vegetables

2	garlic bulbs, cloves separated
2	russet potatoes, cut into quarters (about 1½ pounds)
3	beets, peeled and cut into halves
8	ounces large mushrooms, cut into halves
8	ounces baby carrots
1	large sweet onion, cut into quarters
⅓	cup olive oil
2	teaspoons dried basil
2	teaspoons dried oregano
½	teaspoon salt
	Pepper to taste
8	ounces fresh green beans, trimmed

Combine the garlic, potatoes, beets, mushrooms, carrots, onion, olive oil, basil, oregano, salt and pepper in a large bowl and toss to mix. Spread in a lightly greased 10×15-inch baking pan. Bake at 450 degrees for 15 minutes. Stir in the beans and bake for 15 minutes longer.

MAKES 4 TO 6 SERVINGS

Vegetarian Red Beans and Dirty Rice

1	teaspoon olive oil
1	cup seven-grain rice blend or brown rice
1/4	cup chopped red onion
2	garlic cloves, minced
1/2	cup finely chopped carrots
1/4	cup chopped celery
1	small jalapeño chile, seeded and minced, or to taste
2	teaspoons cumin
2	teaspoons coriander
1	teaspoon chili powder
2	cups vegetable stock
1/2	bay leaf
1	(16-ounce) can red beans, drained and rinsed
3/4	cup chopped tomatoes
1/4	cup fresh or frozen corn kernels
1/2	teaspoon sea salt
1	tablespoon chopped fresh parsley
1	tablespoon chopped fresh cilantro

Heat the olive oil in a large saucepan. Add the rice, onion, garlic, carrots, celery, jalapeño chile, cumin, coriander and chili powder and sauté for 3 to 5 minutes or until the mixture is light brown. Bring the stock and bay leaf to a boil in a saucepan. Stir into the rice mixture and reduce the heat. Simmer, covered, for 15 minutes. Stir in the beans, tomatoes, corn and salt. Simmer, covered, for 15 minutes or until the liquid is absorbed. Remove from the heat and stir in the parsley and cilantro. Remove the bay leaf before serving.

MAKES 4 SERVINGS

Mexican Vegetarian Casserole

1	*(15-ounce) can whole kernel corn, drained*
1	*(15-ounce) can black beans, drained and rinsed*
1	*(10-ounce) can tomatoes with green chiles*
1	*cup sour cream*
1	*(8-ounce) jar picante sauce*
2	*cups (8 ounces) shredded Cheddar cheese*
2	*cups cooked rice*
1/4	*teaspoon pepper*
6	*green onions, chopped*
1	*(2-ounce) can sliced black olives*
2	*cups (8 ounces) shredded Monterey Jack cheese*

Combine the corn, beans, tomatoes with green chiles, sour cream, picante sauce, Cheddar cheese, rice and pepper in a bowl and mix well. Spoon into a lightly greased 9×13-inch baking dish. Sprinkle with the green onions, olives and Monterey Jack cheese. Bake at 350 degrees for 50 minutes.

MAKES 6 SERVINGS

SAVE ROOM FOR DESSERT

⸗

Cakes, Pies, and Cookies

Almond Pound Cake

1½	cups (3 sticks) butter, softened	1	teaspoon vanilla extract
8	ounces cream cheese, softened	2	teaspoons almond extract
3	cups sugar	6	eggs
	Dash of salt	3	cups all-purpose flour

Beat the butter and cream cheese in a mixing bowl until light and fluffy. Beat in the sugar gradually. Beat in the salt, vanilla and almond extract. Add the eggs one at a time, beating well after each addition. Beat in the flour, one cup at a time. Pour into a greased and floured 10-inch tube pan. Bake at 325 degrees for 1 hour and 10 minutes or until the cake tests done. Let cool in the pan for 10 minutes. Invert onto a wire rack to cool completely. Remove to a serving plate and store in an airtight container.

MAKES 16 SERVINGS

Cherry Pound Cake

3	cups all-purpose flour	1	tablespoon vanilla extract
1	teaspoon baking powder	1	cup sour cream
½	teaspoon baking soda	6	egg whites, stiffly beaten
1	cup (2 sticks) butter, softened	½	cup chopped drained
3	cups sugar		maraschino cherries
6	egg yolks		

Sift the flour, baking powder and baking soda together. Beat the butter and sugar in a mixing bowl until light and fluffy. Add the egg yolks and vanilla and beat for 3 minutes. Beat in the dry ingredients. Add the sour cream and beat for 3 minutes. Fold in the egg whites and cherries with a rubber spatula. Pour into a greased 9-inch tube pan. Bake at 350 degrees for 60 to 70 minutes or until the cake tests done. Check after 30 minutes of baking and cover the top with foil if becoming too brown. Cool in the pan for 10 minutes. Remove to a wire rack to cool completely.

MAKES 15 SERVINGS

PHOTO ON PAGE 151

Coffee Cream Cake

CAKE

3	cups sifted all-purpose flour
1	teaspoon baking soda
1	teaspoon baking powder
4	teaspoons baking cocoa
1	cup shortening
2 1/2	cups sugar
5	egg yolks
1	cup buttermilk
5	tablespoons strong brewed coffee
2	tablespoons vanilla extract
5	egg whites, beaten

MOCHA ICING

1/2	cup (1 stick) butter, softened
2	egg yolks, or 1 egg
2	teaspoons baking cocoa
3 3/4	cups confectioners' sugar
1	tablespoon strong brewed coffee
1	teaspoon vanilla extract

CAKE

Mix the flour, baking soda, baking powder and baking cocoa together. Beat the shortening and sugar in a mixing bowl until light and fluffy. Beat in the egg yolks. Beat in the buttermilk. Beat in the dry ingredients gradually. Beat in the coffee and vanilla. Fold in the egg whites. Pour into three greased and floured 9-inch cake pans. Bake at 325 degrees for 25 to 30 minutes or until the cakes test done. Cool in the pans for 10 minutes. Remove to a wire rack to cool completely.

ICING

Beat the butter, egg yolks, baking cocoa, confectioners' sugar, coffee and vanilla in a mixing bowl until smooth. Spread between the layers and over the top and side of the cooled cake.

Note: If you are concerned about using raw eggs, use eggs pasteurized in their shells, which are sold at some specialty food stores, or use an equivalent amount of pasteurized egg yolks or pasteurized egg substitute in the icing

MAKES 12 TO 16 SERVINGS

Milky Way Cake

CAKE

3	eggs
1½	cups sugar
2	cups all-purpose flour
½	teaspoon vanilla extract
	Pinch of salt
2	teaspoons dark corn syrup
2	ounces semisweet chocolate, melted
½	cup (1 stick) butter, melted
1	cup buttermilk

CHOCOLATE FROSTING

¼	cup (½ stick) butter, softened
1 to 1¼	(16-ounce) packages confectioners' sugar, sifted
3	tablespoons baking cocoa
4½	teaspoons heavy cream

CAKE

Combine the eggs, sugar, flour, vanilla, salt, corn syrup, chocolate, butter and buttermilk in a bowl and mix well. Pour into two greased and floured 8-inch cake pans. Bake at 350 degrees for 30 minutes or until the cakes test done. Cool in the pans for 10 minutes. Remove to a wire rack to cool completely. Cut each layer in half horizontally with a serrated knife or unflavored dental floss to make four layers.

FROSTING

Beat the butter, confectioners' sugar and cocoa in a bowl. Add the cream and beat until smooth, adding a few more drops of cream if the frosting is too stiff. Spread between the layers and over the top and side of the cooled cake.

MAKES 12 TO 16 SERVINGS

Dark Chocolate Cake

1	(2-layer) package dark chocolate cake mix
1	(3-ounce) package chocolate instant pudding mix
2	cups sour cream
3	eggs
1/3	cup vegetable oil
1/2	cup coffee-flavored liqueur
2	cups (12 ounces) semisweet chocolate chips
	Baking cocoa
	Confectioners' sugar

Beat the cake mix, pudding mix, sour cream, eggs, oil and liqueur in a mixing bowl. Fold in the chocolate chips; the batter will be very thick. Pour into a greased 10-inch bundt pan dusted with baking cocoa. Bake at 350 degrees for 1 hour or until the cake tests done. Cool in the pan for 10 to 15 minutes. Invert onto a wire rack. Dust with confectioners' sugar and serve warm with whipped cream.

MAKES 16 SERVINGS

Pig Trail Cake

1	cup chopped pecans
1	cup flaked coconut
1	(2-layer) package German chocolate cake mix
1/3	cup vegetable oil
3	eggs
8	ounces cream cheese, softened
1/2	cup (1 stick) butter, softened
3 3/4	cups confectioners' sugar

Spread the pecans and coconut over the bottom of a greased 9×13-inch baking dish. Combine the cake mix, oil and eggs in a bowl and mix according to the package directions. Pour over the pecans and coconut. Combine the cream cheese, butter and confectioners' sugar and mix well. Drop by tablespoonfuls evenly over the batter. Bake at 325 degrees for 1 hour. Remove to a wire rack to cool.

MAKES 15 SERVINGS

Infinity Liqueur Cake

CAKE

1	(2-layer) package yellow cake mix
1	(3-ounce) package vanilla instant pudding mix
4	eggs
1/2	cup vegetable oil
1/2	cup cold water
1/2	cup favorite liqueur, such as amaretto, apricot brandy, orange-flavored liqueur, rum or whiskey

LIQUEUR GLAZE

1/2	cup (1 stick) butter
1/4	cup water
1	cup sugar
1/2	cup favorite liqueur, such as amaretto, apricot brandy, orange-flavored liqueur, rum or whiskey

CAKE

Beat the cake mix, pudding mix, eggs, oil, water and liqueur in a mixing bowl. Pour into a greased and floured bundt pan. Bake at 325 degrees for 55 minutes or until the cake tests done. Remove to a wire rack to cool completely. Invert onto a serving plate and poke holes over the top and side of the cake with a fork or wooden pick.

GLAZE

Melt the butter in a saucepan over medium heat. Stir in the water and sugar. Bring to a boil and boil for 5 minutes, stirring constantly. Remove from the heat and stir in the liqueur. Drizzle a small amount of the glaze over the cake, allowing it to soak in before adding more glaze. Repeat using all of the glaze.

MAKES 16 SERVINGS

German Chocolate Cake

CAKE

2	cups all-purpose flour
1	teaspoon baking soda
1/4	teaspoon salt
4	ounces German's sweet chocolate
1/2	cup water
1	cup (2 sticks) butter, softened
2	cups sugar
4	egg yolks
1	teaspoon vanilla extract
1	cup buttermilk
4	egg whites, stiffly beaten

COCONUT PECAN FROSTING

1	cup evaporated milk
1	cup sugar
3	egg yolks
1/2	cup (1 stick) butter
1	teaspoon vanilla extract
1	cup chopped pecans
2	cups flaked coconut

CAKE

Mix the flour, baking soda and salt together. Combine the chocolate and water in a microwave-safe bowl. Microwave on High until the chocolate is almost melted, stirring once. Beat the butter and sugar in a mixing bowl at medium speed until light and fluffy. Add the egg yolks one at a time, beating well after each addition. Beat in the chocolate mixture and vanilla. Beat in the dry ingredients alternately with the buttermilk, beating well after each addition. Fold in the egg whites. Pour into two greased and floured 9-inch cake pans lined with baking parchment. Bake at 350 degrees for 30 minutes or until wooden picks inserted in the centers come out clean. Run a thin knife around the edge of the pans and let cool in the pans for 15 minutes. Remove to a wire rack and remove the baking parchment. Let cool completely.

FROSTING

Combine the evaporated milk, sugar, egg yolks, butter and vanilla in a heavy saucepan. Cook over low heat until thick, stirring constantly. Remove from the heat and stir in the pecans and coconut. Let cool to room temperature. Spread between the layers and over the top and side of the cooled cake.

MAKES 12 TO 16 SERVINGS

Mary Frances George's Waldorf Red Cake

CAKE

- 1/2   cup (1 stick) butter, softened
- 1 1/2 cups sugar
- 2   eggs
- 1/4   cup red food color
- 1   tablespoon baking cocoa
- 1   teaspoon salt
- 1   teaspoon vanilla extract
- 2 1/4 cups sifted cake flour
- 1   cup buttermilk
- 1   teaspoon baking soda
- 1   teaspoon vinegar

BUTTER ICING

- 1   cup milk
- 5   tablespoons all-purpose flour
- 1   cup (2 sticks) butter, softened
- 2   cups confectioners' sugar
- 1   tablespoon vanilla extract

CAKE

Beat the butter and sugar in a mixing bowl until light and fluffy. Add the eggs and beat well. Mix the food color and baking cocoa in a bowl to make a paste. Add to the butter mixture and beat well. Beat in the salt and vanilla. Beat in the flour alternately with the buttermilk. Mix the baking soda and vinegar in a bowl. Add to the batter and mix just until blended. Pour into two greased and floured 9-inch cake pans. Bake at 350 degrees for 30 to 35 minutes or until the cakes test done. Cool in the pans for 10 minutes. Remove to a wire rack to cool completely. Cut each layer in half horizontally with a serrated knife or unflavored dental floss to make four layers.

ICING

Stir the milk gradually into the flour in a saucepan. Cook until very thick, stirring constantly. Remove from the heat and let cool completely. Remove to a mixing bowl. Add the butter, confectioners' sugar and vanilla and beat until very creamy. Spread between the layers and over the top and side of the cooled cake.

MAKES 12 TO 16 SERVINGS

Tontitown Cream Cake

CAKE

2	cups all-purpose flour
1	teaspoon baking soda
1/2	cup shortening
1/2	cup (1 stick) butter, softened
2	cups sugar
5	egg yolks
1	cup buttermilk
1	teaspoon vanilla extract
1	(7-ounce) can flaked coconut
1	cup chopped pecans
5	egg whites, stiffly beaten

CREAM CHEESE ICING

1/4	cup (1/2 stick) butter, softened
8	ounces cream cheese, softened
3 3/4	cups confectioners' sugar
1	teaspoon vanilla extract
	Toasted flaked coconut (optional)

CAKE

Mix the flour and baking soda together. Beat the shortening and butter in a mixing bowl until light and fluffy. Beat in the sugar. Add the egg yolks and beat well. Beat in the dry ingredients alternately with the buttermilk. Beat in the vanilla, coconut and pecans. Fold in the egg whites. Pour into three greased and floured 9-inch cake pans. Bake at 350 degrees for 25 minutes or until the cakes test done. Cool in the pans for 10 minutes. Remove to a wire rack to cool completely.

ICING

Beat the butter and cream cheese in a bowl until light and fluffy. Add the confectioners' sugar and vanilla and beat until smooth. Spread between the layers and over the top and side of the cooled cake. Sprinkle with coconut.

MAKES 12 TO 16 SERVINGS

The history of Tontitown begins with the story of immigrants. Faced with high taxes and political unrest, a group of Italian farming families came to the United States in 1895. After a false start in southeast Arkansas, Father Pietro Bandini bought a plot of land in Northwest Arkansas and brought some forty families here. They named the colony Tontitown for Henri de Tonti, LaSalle's chief lieutenant. Every August since 1899, the thriving community celebrates Tontitown's Italian heritage with the annual Tontitown Grape Festival.

Pat Walker's Watergate Cake

1   *(2-layer) package white cake mix*
3   *eggs*
3/4   *cup vegetable oil*
1/2   *cup chopped nuts*
1   *(3-ounce) package pistachio instant pudding mix*
1   *cup lemon-lime soda, at room temperature*
1/2   *cup flaked coconut*
1   *teaspoon coconut flavoring*
1   *(3-ounce) package pistachio instant pudding mix*
8   *ounces whipped topping*

Combine the cake mix, eggs, oil, nuts, 1 package pudding mix, the lemon-lime soda, coconut and coconut flavoring in a bowl and mix well. Pour into a greased 9×13-inch cake pan. Bake according to the cake mix package directions. Remove to a wire rack to cool completely. Stir 1 package pudding mix into the whipped topping in a bowl. Spread over the cooled cake. Chill until ready to serve.

MAKES 15 SERVINGS

Debbie Walker's Cola Cake

2   *cups all-purpose flour*
2   *cups sugar*
1   *teaspoon baking soda*
1   *cup cola*
1   *cup (2 sticks) butter*
1/4   *cup baking cocoa*

1 1/2 *cups miniature marshmallows*
1/2   *cup buttermilk*
2   *eggs, beaten*
1   *teaspoon vanilla extract*
       Cola Icing (page 161)

Sift the flour, sugar and baking soda into a large bowl. Bring the cola, butter and baking cocoa to a boil in a saucepan, stirring occasionally. Remove from the heat and add the marshmallows. Stir until the marshmallows are melted. Stir in the buttermilk, eggs and vanilla. Make a well in the dry ingredients. Add the cola mixture and mix well. Pour into a greased and floured 10×15-inch cake pan or 9×13-inch cake pan. Bake at 350 degrees for 20 to 30 minutes or until the cake tests done. Remove to a wire rack and let cool slightly. Pour Cola Icing over the warm cake. Let cool before serving.

MAKES 15 SERVINGS

Cola Icing

½	cup (1 stick) butter
3	tablespoons baking cocoa
6	tablespoons cola
1	(16-ounce) package confectioners' sugar

Bring the butter, baking cocoa and cola to a boil in a saucepan, stirring frequently. Remove from the heat and whisk in the confectioners' sugar until smooth.

MAKES 15 SERVINGS

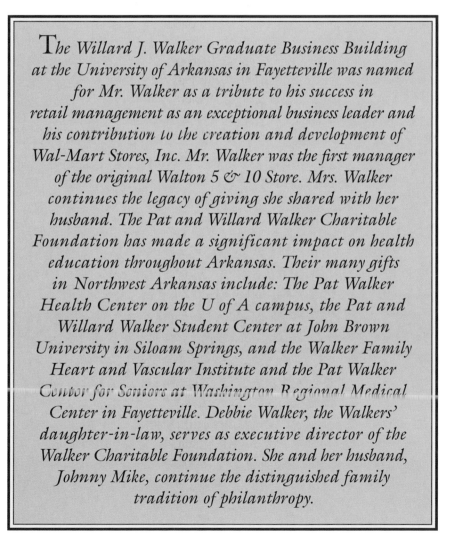

The Willard J. Walker Graduate Business Building at the University of Arkansas in Fayetteville was named for Mr. Walker as a tribute to his success in retail management as an exceptional business leader and his contribution to the creation and development of Wal-Mart Stores, Inc. Mr. Walker was the first manager of the original Walton 5 & 10 Store. Mrs. Walker continues the legacy of giving she shared with her husband. The Pat and Willard Walker Charitable Foundation has made a significant impact on health education throughout Arkansas. Their many gifts in Northwest Arkansas include: The Pat Walker Health Center on the U of A campus, the Pat and Willard Walker Student Center at John Brown University in Siloam Springs, and the Walker Family Heart and Vascular Institute and the Pat Walker Center for Seniors at Washington Regional Medical Center in Fayetteville. Debbie Walker, the Walkers' daughter-in-law, serves as executive director of the Walker Charitable Foundation. She and her husband, Johnny Mike, continue the distinguished family tradition of philanthropy.

New Zealand Ricotta Cake

1¼ cups ricotta cheese
2   eggs
    Grated zest and juice of 1 orange
¾   cup olive oil
¾   cup milk
1¼ cups sugar
2   cups self-rising flour
1   cup blueberries
    Sugar

Beat the cheese, eggs, orange zest, orange juice, olive oil, milk and 1¼ cups sugar in a mixing bowl. Add the flour and mix well. Pour into a greased deep 12-inch baking dish. Arrange the blueberries on top and sprinkle with sugar. Bake at 325 degrees for 40 minutes or until set. Remove to a wire rack to cool.

MAKES 8 SERVINGS

Pumpkin Pie Cake

1   (29-ounce) can pumpkin
4   eggs
13 ounces evaporated milk
1½ cups sugar
1   tablespoon cinnamon
1   teaspoon ginger
½   teaspoon nutmeg
1   (2-layer) package yellow cake mix
1   cup (2 sticks) butter, melted
1   cup chopped pecans
    Whipped cream for garnish

Beat the pumpkin, eggs, evaporated milk, sugar, cinnamon, ginger and nutmeg in a mixing bowl. Pour into a greased 9×13-inch cake pan. Sprinkle the dry cake mix evenly over the top. Pour the butter evenly over the cake mix and sprinkle with the pecans. Bake at 350 degrees for 1 hour. Remove to a wire rack to cool completely. Cut into squares and garnish with whipped cream.

MAKES 15 SERVINGS

Chocolate Cobbler

1/2	cup (1 stick) butter
1 1/2	cups sugar
3	tablespoons baking cocoa
2	cups self-rising flour
1	cup milk
2	teaspoons vanilla extract
2	cups sugar
1/2	cup baking cocoa
3	cups boiling water

Melt the butter in a 9×13-inch baking pan in the oven and tilt the pan to coat the bottom. Combine 1 1/2 cups sugar, 3 tablespoons baking cocoa, the flour, milk and vanilla in a bowl and mix well. Spoon evenly into the prepared pan. Mix 2 cups sugar and 1/2 cup baking cocoa in a bowl and sprinkle over the batter. Pour the boiling water evenly over the top; do not stir. Bake at 350 degrees for 30 to 40 minutes or until the top is firm. Serve warm with ice cream or whipped cream.

MAKES 15 SERVINGS

Orange Zabaglione

5	egg yolks
1	egg
5	tablespoons sugar
1/2	cup orange juice
1	tablespoon sherry
1/2	cup heavy whipping cream, whipped (optional)

Whisk the egg yolks, egg, sugar, orange juice and sherry in the top of a double boiler until light and creamy. Place over simmering water. Cook for 10 minutes or until thickened, whisking constantly. The mixture will foam up before thickening. Pour into six glasses and serve immediately or place the top of the double boiler over a bowl of cool water and whisk until cool. Fold in the whipped cream and chill until ready to serve.

MAKES 6 SERVINGS

Johnelle Hunt's Glazed Apple Pie

Mrs. Hunt shared that "this apple pie is a family favorite. I taught my son, Bryan, how to make it and now his turns out better than mine!"

2	cups all-purpose flour	6	cups sliced apples
1	teaspoon salt	3	tablespoons margarine,
3/4	cup shortening		cut into pieces
1/4	cup ice water	2	tablespoons orange juice
3/4	cup granulated sugar	1	teaspoon grated orange zest
2	tablespoons all-purpose flour	3	tablespoons orange juice
1/2	teaspoon cinnamon	1	cup confectioners' sugar
1/8	teaspoon salt		

Mix 2 cups flour and 1 teaspoon salt in a bowl. Cut in the shortening with a pastry blender or fork until crumbly. Add the water gradually and stir just until the mixture forms a dough. Shape the dough into a ball and divide in half. Roll out each half into a 12-inch circle on a floured work surface. Fit one circle in a 9-inch pie plate. Combine the granulated sugar, 2 tablespoons flour, the cinnamon and 1/8 teaspoon salt in a bowl and mix well. Add the apples and toss to coat. Spoon into the pastry-lined pie plate and dot the top with the margarine. Sprinkle with 2 tablespoons orange juice. Top with the remaining pastry, crimping the edges and cutting vents. Bake at 400 degrees for 40 minutes. Remove to a wire rack. Combine the orange zest, 3 tablespoons orange juice and the confectioners' sugar in a bowl and mix well. Spread over the hot pie. Let cool before serving.

MAKES 6 TO 8 SERVINGS

The story of Johnelle and J. B. Hunt is one of hard work and perseverance, combined with family values and an uncanny business sense. J. B. Hunt Transport Services, Inc., located in Lowell, began in 1969 with five trucks and seven trailers. Today it is the largest publicly held truckload transportation company in North America. The Hunts have a generous history of giving in Northwest Arkansas and throughout the state. Major gifts have been given to Mercy Health of Northwest Arkansas, Washington Regional Medical Center, and the University of Arkansas, among others.

Devil's Den Fudge Pie

1 cup sugar
1/4 cup all-purpose flour
1/4 cup baking cocoa
1/2 cup (1 stick) butter, melted
2 eggs
1 teaspoon vanilla extract
1 unbaked (8-inch) pie shell

Mix the sugar, flour and baking cocoa in a bowl. Add the butter and mix well. Add the eggs and vanilla and mix until smooth. Pour into the pie shell. Bake at 325 degrees for 30 to 35 minutes or until set. Remove to a wire rack. Serve warm with ice cream or whipped cream.

MAKES 8 SERVINGS

Impossible Coconut Pie

1 3/4 cups sugar
1/2 cup self-rising flour
4 eggs, well beaten
2 cups milk
4 tablespoons butter, melted
1 teaspoon vanilla extract
Pinch of salt
2 cups flaked coconut

Mix the sugar and flour together. Combine the eggs, milk, butter, vanilla, salt and coconut in a bowl and mix well. Add the dry ingredients and mix well. Pour into a well-greased 10-inch pie plate. Bake at 375 degrees for 45 minutes; the center will set as it cools. Remove to a wire rack to cool completely.

MAKES 8 SERVINGS

Coffee Toffee Pie

CRUST

1	cup all-purpose flour
1/4	cup packed light brown sugar
1	ounce unsweetened chocolate, grated
1/4	cup (1/2 stick) butter
2	tablespoons (or more) milk
1	teaspoon vanilla extract
3/4	cup walnuts, finely chopped

FILLING

1/2	cup (1 stick) butter, softened
3/4	cup sugar
2	teaspoons instant coffee granules
1	ounce unsweetened chocolate, melted
2	eggs

TOPPING

1 1/2	cups cold heavy whipping cream
6	tablespoons confectioners' sugar
4 1/2	teaspoons instant coffee granules
	Chocolate curls for garnish

CRUST

Mix the flour, brown sugar and grated chocolate in a bowl. Cut in the butter with a pastry blender, fork or your fingers until crumbly. Add the milk, vanilla and walnuts and mix well. Add a few additional drops of milk if the dough is too dry or chill until firm if the dough is sticky. Press the dough over the bottom and up the side of a 9-inch pie plate. Crimp the edge with a fork dipped in flour. Prick the dough all over with a fork. Press a 12-inch square of heavy-duty foil against the bottom and side of the pie shell. Bake at 375 degrees for 8 minutes. Remove the foil and bake for 10 minutes longer or until the crust is dry and crisp. Remove to a wire rack to cool completely.

FILLING

Beat the butter in a mixing bowl until light and fluffy. Beat in the sugar gradually at high speed. Beat in the coffee granules and chocolate. Add the eggs one at a time, beating at high speed for 5 minutes after each addition. Spread the filling into the cooled pie shell. Chill, covered, for at least 6 hours.

TOPPING

Beat the cream, confectioners' sugar and coffee granules at high speed in a mixing bowl until stiff peaks form. Dollop the whipped cream mixture around the edge of the pie and garnish with a few chocolate curls in the center. Chill for at least 2 hours.

Note: If you are concerned about using raw eggs, use eggs pasteurized in their shells, which are sold at some specialty food stores, or use an equivalent amount of pasteurized egg substitute.

MAKES 10 SERVINGS

Bernice Jones's Bridge Club Pie

1   *(14-ounce) can sweetened condensed milk*
3   *tablespoons lemon juice*
9   *ounces whipped topping*
1   *(15-ounce) can crushed pineapple, drained*
1   *cup chopped nuts*
1   *(9-inch) graham cracker pie shell*
     Maraschino cherries or chopped nuts for garnish

Combine the condensed milk and lemon juice in a bowl and mix well. Fold in the whipped topping, pineapple and 1 cup nuts. Spread into the pie shell and garnish with maraschino cherries or chopped nuts. Chill until ready to serve.

MAKES 6 TO 8 SERVINGS

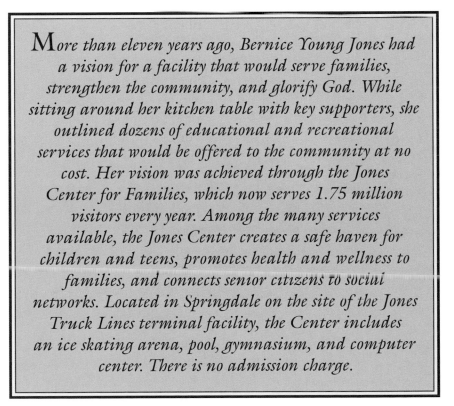

More than eleven years ago, Bernice Young Jones had a vision for a facility that would serve families, strengthen the community, and glorify God. While sitting around her kitchen table with key supporters, she outlined dozens of educational and recreational services that would be offered to the community at no cost. Her vision was achieved through the Jones Center for Families, which now serves 1.75 million visitors every year. Among the many services available, the Jones Center creates a safe haven for children and teens, promotes health and wellness to families, and connects senior citizens to social networks. Located in Springdale on the site of the Jones Truck Lines terminal facility, the Center includes an ice skating arena, pool, gymnasium, and computer center. There is no admission charge.

Cranberry Raisin Pie

12	ounces (3 cups) fresh cranberries
3/4	cup raisins
1 1/2	cups sugar
2	tablespoons all-purpose flour
1	teaspoon cinnamon
2	tablespoons water
1	(2-crust) pie pastry
1/4	cup (1/2 stick) butter, cut into pieces
	Vanilla ice cream

Combine the cranberries, raisins, sugar, flour, cinnamon and water in a bowl and toss to mix. Fit one pastry in an 8- or 9-inch pie plate. Spoon the cranberry mixture into the pie shell. Dot the top with the butter. Cut the remaining pastry into strips. Arrange lattice-fashion over the pie. Bake at 350 degrees until bubbly and the pastry is light brown. Remove to a wire rack to cool. Serve with vanilla ice cream.

MAKES 6 TO 8 SERVINGS

Eggnog Pumpkin Pie

3/4	cup sugar
2	teaspoons cinnamon
1	teaspoon pumpkin pie spice
1/2	teaspoon salt
2	eggs
1	(15-ounce) can pumpkin
1 1/2	cups nonalcoholic eggnog
1	unbaked (9-inch) pie shell, chilled

Mix the sugar, cinnamon, pie spice and salt together. Beat the eggs lightly in a bowl. Stir in the sugar mixture. Add the pumpkin and mix well. Stir in the eggnog. Pour into the pie shell. Bake at 375 degrees for 15 minutes or until the crust is beginning to brown. Reduce the heat to 325 degrees and bake for 40 to 45 minutes or until the crust is golden brown and a wooden pick inserted near the center comes out clean. Remove to a wire rack to cool completely. Serve with whipped cream.

MAKES 8 SERVINGS

Oatmeal Crisps

1	cup (2 sticks) butter, softened
1	cup packed brown sugar
1	cup granulated sugar
2	eggs
1	teaspoon vanilla extract
1½	cups all-purpose flour
1	teaspoon baking soda
1	teaspoon salt
3	cups quick-cooking oats
½	cup finely chopped pecans

Beat the butter, brown sugar and granulated sugar in a mixing bowl until light and fluffy. Beat in the eggs and vanilla. Add the flour, baking soda, salt, oats and pecans and mix well. Shape the dough into tightly-packed logs. Wrap in plastic wrap and chill overnight. Cut the logs into ½-inch-thick slices and arrange on a nonstick cookie sheet. Bake at 350 degrees until light brown. Cool on the cookie sheet for 2 minutes. Remove to a wire rack to cool completely.

MAKES 6 DOZEN

Sugar Pecan Crisps

1½	cups (3 sticks) butter, softened
2	eggs
1⅓	cups sugar
2	teaspoons vanilla extract
3½	cups all-purpose flour
½	teaspoon salt
1	cup finely chopped pecans

Beat the butter, eggs, sugar and vanilla in a mixing bowl until light and fluffy. Add the flour, salt and pecans and mix well. Shape the dough into logs. Wrap in waxed paper and chill for 4 hours. Cut the logs into thin slices and arrange on a nonstick cookie sheet. Bake at 350 degrees for 15 to 20 minutes. Cool on the cookie sheet for 2 minutes. Remove to a wire rack to cool completely.

MAKES 8 DOZEN

Chewy Brownies

1	cup (2 sticks) butter
6	tablespoons baking cocoa
2	cups sugar
2	eggs, beaten
1	cup all-purpose flour
1	teaspoon vanilla extract
1	cup chopped nuts (optional)

Combine the butter and baking cocoa in the top of a double boiler over simmering water. Cook until the butter is melted, stirring frequently. Remove the mixture to a bowl. Stir in the sugar and eggs quickly. Fold in the flour, vanilla and nuts. Pour into a buttered 8×8-inch or 9×9-inch baking pan. Bake at 300 degrees for 45 to 50 minutes; do not overbake. Remove to a wire rack and let cool for 1 hour. Cut into squares.

MAKES 12 SERVINGS

Popcorn Balls

1	cup sugar
1/4	cup dark corn syrup
1/4	cup water
1/2	teaspoon vinegar
2	tablespoons butter
1/8	teaspoon baking soda
1/2	teaspoon vanilla extract
8	cups popped popcorn

Combine the sugar, corn syrup, water and vinegar in a saucepan and mix well. Cook over low heat until the sugar is dissolved, stirring constantly. Bring to a boil and cook to 260 degrees on a candy thermometer, hard-ball stage; do not stir. Add the butter and cook until the mixture spins a thread when dropped from a spoon, stirring occasionally. Remove from the heat and stir in the baking soda and vanilla. Pour over the popcorn in a large bowl and mix quickly. Shape into balls with your buttered hands. Store in an airtight container when cool.

MAKES 8 SERVINGS

No-Bake Fruitcake

1/4	cup grape juice
1	cup heavy whipping cream, whipped
32	large marshmallows, cut into bite-size pieces
1	cup golden raisins
1	cup dried currants
24	ounces graham crackers
1/2	teaspoon cinnamon
1/2	teaspoon nutmeg
1	cup chopped dates
2	cups chopped pecans
1/4	cup chopped figs
1/2	cup diced candied pineapple
3/4	cup candied cherries
1/4	cup diced citron
2	tablespoons grated orange zest
1/4	cup brandy (optional)
6 to	8 red and green candied cherries for garnish

Fold the grape juice into the whipped cream in a bowl. Fold in the marshmallows.
Let stand for the flavors to blend. Cover the raisins and currants with boiling
water in a shallow bowl. Let stand for 10 minutes; drain and pat dry with a paper
towel. Process the graham crackers to a fine powder in a food processor. Remove
to a large bowl. Add the cinnamon and nutmeg and mix well. Add the dates, pecans,
figs, pineapple, 3/4 cup cherries, the citron and orange zest and mix well. Add the
raisins and currants and mix well. Fold in the marshmallow mixture. Fold in the brandy.
Press the mixture into a greased bundt pan. Unmold onto waxed paper and press
candied cherries onto the top. Refrigerate in a sealed tin or airtight cake carrier for
3 to 4 weeks before serving.

MAKES 15 SERVINGS

Best Frosting Ever

2   cups shortening
1   teaspoon salt
1   teaspoon vanilla extract
1   teaspoon almond extract
3   pounds confectioners' sugar
1   cup evaporated milk
     Food color (optional)

Beat the shortening, salt, vanilla and almond extract at high speed in a mixing bowl. Beat in the confectioners' sugar alternately with the evaporated milk and beat until creamy. Beat in food color, a few drops at a time, to the desired tint.

MAKES ABOUT 8 CUPS

Hot Fudge Sauce

1/2   cup baking cocoa
3/4   cup sugar
1/2   cup evaporated milk
1/3   cup light corn syrup
5 1/3 tablespoons butter
1   teaspoon vanilla extract

Mix the baking cocoa and sugar in a saucepan. Stir in the evaporated milk and corn syrup. Bring to a boil over medium heat, stirring constantly. Boil for 1 minute, stirring constantly. Remove from the heat and add the butter and vanilla. Stir until the butter is melted. Serve over ice cream.

MAKES 2 CUPS

Grape Goodness

1	cup sour cream
8	ounces cream cheese, softened
1/4	cup granulated sugar
2	teaspoons vanilla extract
2	pounds seedless red grapes
2	pounds seedless green grapes
1	cup packed brown sugar
2	cups chopped pecans or walnuts

Combine the sour cream, cream cheese, granulated sugar and vanilla in a large mixing bowl and beat until smooth and creamy. Fold in the grapes.

Spread the grape mixture in a 9×13-inch dish. Sprinkle with the brown sugar and pecans. Chill, covered, until serving time.

MAKES 8 SERVINGS

Chocolate Chip Tea Cakes

1	cup (2 sticks) butter, softened
1/2	cup sifted confectioners' sugar
1	teaspoon vanilla extract
2	cups all-purpose flour
2/3	cup finely chopped walnuts or pecans
2	cups (12 ounces) semisweet chocolate chips

Beat the butter and confectioners' sugar in a large mixing bowl until creamy. Beat in the vanilla. Add the flour and walnuts gradually, beating constantly until combined. Stir in 1 1/2 cups of the chocolate chips.

Shape the dough into 1-inch balls and arrange the balls 2 inches apart on an ungreased baking sheet. Bake at 350 degrees for 10 to 12 minutes or until set or golden brown on the edges. Cool on the baking sheet for 10 minutes and then remove to a wire rack to cool completely.

Place the remaining 1/2 cup chocolate chips in a heavy-duty sealable plastic bag. Microwave for 30 seconds and knead the bag. Microwave at additional 20-second intervals, kneading after each interval until smooth. Cut a tiny corner in the bag and drizzle the chocolate over the tea cakes. Chill the tea cakes for 5 minutes or until the chocolate is set. Store in an airtight container at room temperature.

MAKES 4 DOZEN

FOUNDERS CIRCLE

Jennifer and Rick Apolskis

Stephanie and Brett Austin

TJ and Bob Bedard

Sarah and Andrew Boyer

Hope and John Bradberry

Kerry and Chris Bradley

Kristen Caldwell

Tiffany and Ragain Chapman

Heather and Rick Ellington

Melissa and Alan Epler

Holly and Marty Gilbert

Andrea Hall

Susan and Anthony Hui

Marla and Dennis Hunt

Becky and Max Koonce

Karen Light

Bettie Luper

Vanessa and Greg Miller

Elise and Raye Mitchell

Dr. Tammy Grammer Morris

Eva Madison and David Pieper

Carin and Marty Schoppmeyer

Courtney and Jim Smith

Stacey and Jan Sturner

Leslee and Brad Urhahn

Kamron and Phil Whitehead

Tina and Jeff Winham

Blake and Wayne Woolsey

Acknowledgments and Credits

Special Thanks To

Sandra Edwards

Amanda and Jim Ed Reed

for graciously allowing the Junior League to photograph your homes.

Christian Alexander

David McKee

Personally Yours (Fayetteville)

Melanie Reeh

Signed, Sealed, Delivered (Rogers)

In Loving Memory of
Those Who Taught and Inspired Us

Mary Barnhart

Josephine Borchelt

Lena Elizabeth Cabe

Linda Cooper

Phyllis Cruz

Pauline Davis

Wanda Hall Fountain

Carolyn Gilbert

Frank Gilbert

Dot Howell

Mamie Jones

Dottie Kern

Charles Leuthen

Margaret McKay

Hattie Murphy

Evelyn Murray

Felix Thomson

Juanita Thomson

Margaret Turchi

Clara Bell Waggoner

Geneva Willems

RECIPE CONTRIBUTORS

Phoebe Adams
Diane Adamson
Johnnie Alley
Emily Anderson
Jennifer Apolskis
Amanda Armour
Jenna Elise Ashbreck
Rosa Atchley
Stephanie Austin
Jo Barnhart
Linda Berry
Melissa Berry
Angela Beshears
Roberta Billingsley
Chelsea K. Blackwell
Lynn Blair
Joyce Blake
Lucille Blake
Jennifer Bohnert
Jennifer Booher
Celia Boon
Karen Boston
Christopher and Tara Brace
Hope Bradberry
Angie Brandenburg
John Brandt
Susie Brandt
Karrie Branson
Kristy Brown
Linda Allen Brown
Pam Brown
Maynon Burson
Kristen Butler
Ruth Campbell
Dortha Carlton
Tiffany Chapman
Mandy Clark
Sallie Clark
Patricia Clinton
Kristen Cobbs
Stacy Cooper
Julie Council
Jordan Covington
William Covington
Zachary Covington

Angela Cox
Jackie Crispens
Pamela Sue Cruz
Dana Proctor Culp
Sarah Curry
Leshia Simone Dockery
Peg Duncan
Bella Dye
Linda Eichmann
Sara Eichmann
Heather Kelley Ellington
Janie Evitts
Barbara Faught
Breanna Adams Faught
Melanie Faught
Alexandria Ferguson
Janice Ferguson
Libby Ferguson
Catherine Fletcher
Kim Fletcher
Virginia Ford
Robin Foshee
Jean Foster
Sandra Fountain
Amber Garton
Amy Gibson
Cara Cathleen Gibson
Betty Gilbert
Courtney Gilbert
Holly Gilbert
Martin Gilbert Sr.
Hope Gillison
Amanda Gittins
Angie Graves
Misty Gulledge
Brenda B. Gullett
Renee Guthrie
Jana Hagge
Sarah Hagge
Ashley Hagler
Judy Hagler
Jennifer Haile
Andrea Hall
Heather Hammons
Linda Hankins

Sheila Hanlon
Leslie Harvey
Sue Haunschild
Ellen Hayward
Peggy Heird
Julie Hewitt
Diane Hirschbach
Kris Honey
Shay Hopper
Jenny House
Liz Hughes
Alexandra Hui
Anthony N. Hui
Jennifer Hui
Mary Margaret Hui
Susan Hui
Victoria Hui
Tom and Judy Humphreys
Deb Hundertmark
Marla Hunt
Amber Hutchinson
Daphne Israel
Mindy Lloyd Jackson
Laura Jacobs
Laura Jensen
Christy Jobe
Mamie Johns
Sara Jouett
Sandra Kellar
Sarah Kellar
Eugene Kelley
Joye Kelley
Shelby Kelley
Friskie Kingrey
Julie Knight
Becky Koonce
JoAnna Krack
Ruth Ann Kunz
Gretchen Laffoon
Emily Lambert
Helen Lampkin
Natalie Larsen
Jeannette Latham
Nancy J. Leake
Elizabeth Lee

Kandy Sue Lee
Karen Light
Pat Lile
Brandy Lindsey
Ethel Lloyd
Jo Long
Lynn Long
Sean Love
Stephanie Love
Caryn Lowe
Bettie Luper
Sherry Lux
Eva C. Madison
Isabelle Mahl
Carol Mainer
Jimmy Elizabeth Martin
Karen Martin
Paula Martucci
Helen Masters
Cammy Jo McCain
Stephanie Smith McCauley
Cindy McDoulett
Scott McDoulett
Lindsay McGarity
Lindsey Tiersa McHenry
Ann McKenzie
Peggy McQueen
Mrs. C. D. McSwain
Janice Meisner
Jodie Kelley Miller
Marsha Miller
Olivia Miller
Vanessa Miller
Lisa Morris
Diane Murphy
Angela Neal
Susan Neyman
Diane Ogden
Michelle Oliver
Paula Parker
Brandie Perry
Kimberly D. Polite
Peggy Polite
Ruby Polite
Teresa Polite

Eddie Polite-Clark
Karen Polite-Nared
Danielle Povar
Lotte Povar
Juliana Price
K. C. Pummill
Antonia Quanstrom
Jamie Ragan
Amanda Ragar
Betty Ragar
Martha Raines
Susan Raines
Wayne Raines
Lorene Raymond
Alynchia Reynolds
LaVaughn Reynolds
Cheryl Ridgeway
Jeanette Roark
Kimberly Roark
Ramona Roberts
Erin Rogers
Jennifer Rokeby-Mayeux
Katie Rowe
Hillary Russell
Ruth Kuhle Ryan
Lara Sandusky
Carin Schoppmeyer
Andrea Sego
Norma Senyard
Holly Shaffer
Margie Sharp
Lepaine Sharp-McHenry
Kebra Shelhamer
Lindsey Shirey
Ashley Kelley Siwiec
Bridgette Smith
Courtney Smith
James Smith
Jeannie Smith
Leslie Harmon Smith
Libby Smith
Caroline Snodgrass
Sarah Solsvig
Joan Starr
Debra Stinchcomb

Lynne Stinson
Vicky Stobaugh
Nancy Stringley
Stephenie Sullivan
Whitney Sutherland
Robin Sutton
Renee Swindell
Courtney Tallmadge
Elizabeth Taylor
Jan Taylor
Mitzi Traxson
Rita Traxson
Kathy Tucker
Christal Tuller
Jaci Uecker
Elvira Urhahn
Leslee Urhahn
Julie Vaught
Kathleen Villar
Tonya Waller
LaVern Watkins
Mary Jane Watkins
Amy Elizabeth Welborn
Lorene Wells
Kamron Whitehead
Pamela Wikstrom
Ceri Marelle Wilkin
Karen Willems
Theresa Willems
Debbie Wintory
Leslie Wintory
Betty Wood
Blake Woolsey
Judy Wright
Kay Wright
Michelle Wynn
Sonya Yates

METRIC EQUIVALENTS

Although the United States has opted to postpone converting to metric measurements, most other countries, including England and Canada, use the metric system. The following chart provides convenient approximate equivalents for allowing use of regular kitchen measures when cooking from foreign recipes.

Volume

These metric measures are approximate
benchmarks for purposes of home food preparation.
1 milliliter = 1 cubic centimeter = 1 gram

Liquid	Dry
1 teaspoon = 5 milliliters	1 quart = 1 liter
1 tablespoon = 15 milliliters	1 ounce = 30 grams
1 fluid ounce = 30 milliliters	1 pound = 450 grams
1 cup = 250 milliliters	2.2 pounds = 1 kilogram
1 pint = 500 milliliters	

Weight	Length
1 ounce = 28 grams	1 inch = 2½ centimeters
1 pound = 450 grams	1/16 inch = 1 millimeter

Formulas Using Conversion Factors

When approximate conversions are not accurate enough, use these
formulas to convert measures from one system to another.

Measurements	Formulas
ounces to grams	# ounces × 28.3 = # grams
grams to ounces	# grams × 0.035 = # ounces
pounds to grams	# pounds × 453.6 = # grams
pounds to kilograms	# pounds × 0.45 = # kilograms
ounces to milliliters	# ounces × 30 = # milliliters
cups to liters	# cups × 0.24 = # liters
inches to centimeters	# inches × 2.54 = # centimeters
centimeters to inches	# centimeters × 0.39 = # inches

Approximate Weight to Volume

Some ingredients which we commonly measure by volume are measured by weight in foreign recipes. Here are a few examples for easy reference.

flour, all-purpose, unsifted	1 pound = 450 grams = 3½ cups
flour, all-purpose, sifted	1 pound = 450 grams = 4 cups
sugar, granulated	1 pound = 450 grams = 2 cups
sugar, brown, packed	1 pound = 450 grams = 2¼ cups
sugar, confectioners', unsifted	1 pound = 450 grams = 4 cups
sugar, confectioners', sifted	1 pound = 450 grams = 4½ cups
butter	1 pound = 450 grams = 2 cups

Temperature

Remember that foreign recipes frequently express temperatures in Centigrade rather than Fahrenheit.

Temperatures	Fahrenheit	Centigrade
room temperature	68°	20°
water boils	212°	100°
baking temperature	350°	177°
baking temperature	375°	190.5°
baking temperature	400°	204.4°
baking temperature	425°	218.3°
baking temperature	450°	232°

Use the following formulas when temperature conversions are necessary.

$$\text{Centigrade degrees} \times \tfrac{9}{5} + 32 = \text{Fahrenheit degrees}$$
$$\text{Fahrenheit degrees} - 32 \times \tfrac{5}{9} = \text{Centigrade degrees}$$

Basic Substitutions

If the recipe calls for	You can substitute:

Flour:

1 cup sifted all-purpose flour	1 cup less 2 tablespoons unsifted all-purpose flour
1 cup sifted cake flour	1 cup less 2 tablespoons sifted all-purpose flour
1 cup sifted self-rising flour	1 cup sifted all-purpose flour plus 1 1/2 teaspoons baking powder and a pinch of salt

Milk/Cream:

1 cup buttermilk	1 cup plain yogurt, or 1 tablespoon lemon juice or vinegar plus enough milk to measure 1 cup—let stand for 5 minutes before using
1 cup whipping cream or half-and-half	7/8 cup whole milk plus 1 1/2 tablespoons butter
1 cup light cream	7/8 cup whole milk plus 3 tablespoons butter
1 cup sour cream	1 cup plain yogurt
1 cup sour milk	1 cup plain yogurt
1 cup whole milk	1 cup skim or nonfat milk plus 2 tablespoons butter or margarine

Seasonings:

1 teaspoon allspice	1/2 teaspoon cinnamon plus 1/8 teaspoon cloves
1 cup ketchup	1 cup tomato sauce plus 1/2 cup sugar plus 2 tablespoons vinegar
1 teaspoon lemon juice	1/2 teaspoon vinegar

Sugar:

1 cup confectioners' sugar	1/2 cup plus 1 tablespoon granulated sugar
1 cup granulated sugar	1 3/4 cups confectioners' sugar, 1 cup packed light brown sugar, or 3/4 cup honey

Other:

1 package active dry yeast	1/2 cake compressed yeast
1 teaspoon baking powder	1/4 teaspoon cream of tartar plus 1/4 teaspoon baking soda
1 cup dry bread crumbs	3/4 cup cracker crumbs, or 1 cup cornflake crumbs
1 cup (2 sticks) butter	7/8 cup vegetable oil, or 1 cup margarine
1 tablespoon cornstarch	2 tablespoons all-purpose flour
1 cup dark corn syrup	3/4 cup light corn syrup plus 1/4 cup light molasses
1 cup light corn syrup	1 cup maple syrup
1 2/3 ounces semisweet chocolate	1 ounce unsweetened chocolate plus 4 teaspoons granulated sugar
1 ounce unsweetened chocolate	3 tablespoons unsweetened baking cocoa plus 1 tablespoon butter or margarine
1 (1-ounce) square chocolate	1/4 cup baking cocoa plus 1 teaspoon shortening
1 cup honey	1 to 1 1/4 cups sugar plus 1/4 cup liquid, or 1 cup corn syrup or molasses
1 egg	1/4 cup mayonnaise

Index

To order additional copies of

ADD ANOTHER PLACE SETTING,

please contact us at:

The Junior League of Northwest Arkansas
614 East Emma, Suite M432
Springdale, AR 72764

OR

at our Web site:

www.juniorleaguenwa.org